FIRST GENERATION

TEN SPEED PRESS
California | New York

FRANKIE GAW

First Generation

Recipes from My Taiwanese-American Home

For my 媽媽 and 爸爸, whom I love so much

For the Asian community, who showed me
my differences were what made me special

For the LGBTQ+ community, which has given
me the freedom to love myself

I will always love you how I do
Let go of a prayer for you
Just a sweet word
The table is prepared for you

—FRANK OCEAN

Contents

RECIPE LIST

Introduction

I AM TAIWANESE AMERICAN. I've grown up with my grandma's steamed pork bao as my favorite food since childhood, yet I've only been to Taiwan twice in my entire life. I can still get excited over a bologna sandwich, fight a stranger over the merits of Olive Garden's breadsticks, and have heart palpitations seeing the green 59A exit sign toward Cracker Barrel and dreaming of their buttered cornbread. And yet, I still get harassed to "go back to my country" and ridiculed for my jet-black hair and tan skin. So where do I belong?

My mom and dad emigrated from Taipei, Taiwan, to Cincinnati, Ohio, in 1985 and never looked back. Like many immigrants before them, they pursued the hope of opportunity, the promise of a better life. Spaghetti and meatballs replaced their childhood comfort of beef noodle soup. Iceberg lettuce with too much ranch dripping down its soggy leaves became their new palate cleanser of choice. The salad was a dish they gleaned from the fanciest restaurant in our neighborhood, Olive Garden, replacing the sweet acidity of lotus roots, fresh ginger, and cucumber of their adolescence. It was a means to adapt to their new life in America.

My parents learned English by watching *Wheel of Fortune,* and after they had me, they worked hours on end to land themselves in corporate America so they could provide the life they dreamed of for their son. For my hard-working parents, time for home cooking was limited, and so the food of my childhood became another avenue for them to raise an all-American kid. It brought McDonald's into my life: Chicken McNuggets for days at a time, enveloping our 1990s Toyota minivan in the smell of fries. Trips to Skyline Chili after soccer practice, where the waitress, who still knows my name twenty years later, would pour a ladle of steaming-hot chili onto chewy spaghetti noodles, sending hints of cinnamon and cumin drifting into my uniform. It was through inconsequential dishes like these, the ones outside of our kitchen, that my love for food and flavor was shaped as I grew up in the suburban Midwest.

1

My relationship with Taiwan didn't begin until later in my childhood, when my two grandmas, who both immigrated to America, became the two Trojan horses of all the things my parents left behind. On visits to my grandma on my dad's side's (nai nai 奶奶) home in Memphis, my morning sweet tooth for Cinnamon Toast Crunch evolved to include a savory craving for the smell of fried oil and greasy scallion pancakes topped with a soft-scrambled egg omelet. When my grandma on my mom's side (po po 婆婆) moved in with us in Ohio, the kitchen island where spaghetti and meatballs once reigned now shared space with pulled noodles vibrantly colored with spinach in a delicate pork and daikon broth. These culinary treasure troves, like those of a lot of immigrant kids, were my secret. They were hidden from view in my day-to-day life of packed Lunchables and PB&Js, only to be enjoyed in the comfort of our family's kitchens.

I didn't start cooking until I was twenty. Until then, I would've proudly described myself as a professional eater but never a cook. My college roommate, Danielle, introduced me to home cooking, delivered serendipitously on a slice of toasted bread with buffalo mozzarella, fresh tomatoes and basil, and a drizzle of balsamic vinegar; I said, "Holy shit! You made that? In our tiny college kitchen?" Of all the things I had consumed up until that point, it was a piece of toast that sparked the idea for me that it was possible to re-create all the flavors I wanted to eat.

As I grew into adulthood, I was living the American Dream in San Francisco, the one my parents had worked so hard to make happen. At twenty-three, I was at the height of my career at Facebook, having just started designing what would become Facebook Live, when my dad began losing his battle to lung cancer. I put my life on hold and went back to Ohio to be with him, knowing he did not have much longer to live. The last thing he wanted to eat was, of all things, fried rice from P.F. Chang's and mooncake from Taiwan that he had stashed in our house. As if morphine was a winter coat, I watched him shed it for a brief moment. When I brought his food over, he regained his appetite like an old friend entering a home on a cold day, eating his final meal that represented both his Lunar New Year as a child and his American guilty pleasure of Chinese takeout, all with a contentment that made me smile.

It took my dad's death for me to begin to look inward to try to understand who I was and where my family came from, using the language I knew best: food. I would fly to Memphis every few months to learn my grandma's recipes, starting with steamed pork buns. I would film her on my iPhone and have my aunt translate the recipes my grandma had scribbled on paper decades ago. After months of learning from my grandma and drawing from the textures and flavors of my own childhood, at age twenty-five, I posted my first photo of a steamed bun to Instagram, acknowledging the pride I felt in my cooking, and most importantly, my Taiwanese roots.

I wanted to write this cookbook to celebrate the first-generation Asian American experience—to reflect on an identity that exists in the in-between, that feeling I've always had of being culturally American yet not white enough, and too American to never feel quite comfortable in my own Taiwanese skin and ancestry. As I've grown up navigating my identity, food has been at the heart of my discovering both deep shame and overflowing pride.

This cookbook is a series of recipes and stories inspired by my family and the resilience of the immigrant spirit. I'll tell about a young girl living in an abandoned mansion in the 1940s. An Asian family who adopts whiteness to survive in suburbia. A millennial who has it all, except his father. Immigrants—their food and their stories—are the heart of America and are what make this country thrive. This is just one of those stories, told by a proud, gay, first-generation Taiwanese American who loves food.

AN AMERICAN PANTRY

I grew up with a distinctly American pantry, a typical coat closet–sized space in suburban Ohio with four wooden shelves, shared by three generations of an immigrant family, under one dinky fluorescent light. My mom used pantry snacks as a tactic: a path for her American son to not only fit in but to out-Gusher and out-Dorito every white kid in the competitive sport that is the school lunch. My dad just wanted a taste of the homeland that he rarely returned to. His contributions included soy-coated rice snack mixes and sesame candy that took him back to Taiwan with every bite. My grandma wanted to nourish her grandson like she had her daughter, filling the remaining shelf space with sesame oils and dried mushrooms with pungent, earthy aromas. Ours was a pantry stocked with sauces, snacks, and ingredients, filled by a family with opposing motivations and cultures. But to me, it didn't feel like a clash; it was just your normal American pantry.

01.

ASIAN MARKET SNACKS

The Asian supermarket is a destination filled with language, color, and smell that feels like a magical world all its own. Every aisle is a gold mine of snacks, many of which enriched my family's pantry when I was growing up. You can view this as a biased guide to eating your way through these very aisles. It's a list of my personal favorites that evoke a nostalgia equally powerful to any American snack I had growing up.

FIG. 01

FIG. 02

FIG. 03

FIG. 04

FIG. 05

FIG. 06

FIG. 07

FIG. 08

SALTY

RICE CRACKERS — *FIG. 01*
Crunchy rice crackers in a variety of shapes, all with a coating of soy and a hint of sweetness

WANT WANT CRACKERS — *FIG. 02*
Puffy rice crackers known for their umami-laden MSG coating

SHRIMP CHIPS — *FIG. 03*
Salty and umami-rich fried chip sticks

KOW KUN BEEF JERKY — *FIG. 04*
An extremely flavorful and tender jerky, not nearly as dry and chewy as American varieties

SOY PEANUTS — *FIG. 05*
Lightly salty peanuts that have been roasted with soy and aromatics

PORK FLOSS — *FIG. 06*
Dehydrated sweet and salty pork jerky, great with congee or rice

DRIED FISH — *FIG. 07*
Briny, salty, and sweet, these crunchy dried fish are the perfect snack on its own or stir-fried in some rice

WASABI PEAS — *FIG. 08*
Crisp sweet peas coated in a crunchy wasabi coating for a bright snack with a kick

SWEET

HELLO PANDA — *FIG. 09*
Thin biscuits shaped like pandas with a creamy filling

POCKY — *FIG. 10*
Crisp biscuit sticks coated in flavor

WHITE RABBIT — *FIG. 11*
A creamy, chewy milk-based candy dream

HAW FLAKES
If fruit roll-ups had a wafer-thin, crispier cousin made of hawthorn berries

YAN YAN — *FIG. 12*
Thick biscuit sticks dipped in sweet frosting

KASUGAI GUMMY CANDIES — *FIG. 13*
(individually wrapped) Chewy and deliciously mouthwatering fruit gummies

ROLLED WAFERS — *FIG. 14*
Crisp and light cookies rolled into long sticks, known for their flakiness

JELLY CUPS — *FIG. 15*
Single-serving shots of fruity gelatin in a plastic cup; lychee and black iced tea are favorites

SESAME AND PEANUT CANDIES — *FIG. 16*
Crisp rectangles of sesame or peanut coated in caramel

BOTAN RICE CANDY — *FIG. 17*
A soft, chewy, citrus-flavored candy wrapped in edible rice-paper

YAKULT — *FIG. 18*
A sweet and tart yogurt drink in a tiny bottle

APPLE SIDRA — *FIG. 19*
A sparkling apple cider soda that's undeniably sweet

RICE PUFF WITH SESAME — *FIG. 20*
A crunch-filled bite of sesame and sweet airy mochi

RAMUNE SOFT DRINK — *FIG. 21*
A Japanese carbonated lemon-citrus drink with a bottle sealed with a marble

YEO'S SOY MILK — *FIG. 22*
A smooth, milky drink made of soy beans that is perfectly sweet

MARUKAWA BUBBLE GUM — *FIG. 23*
Mini bubble gum balls sold in a variety pack of delicious fruit flavors. Hot tip: eat an entire box at once

FIG. 09

FIG. 10

FIG. 11

FIG. 12

FIG. 13

FIG. 14

FIG. 15

FIG. 16

FIG. 17

FIG. 18

FIG. 19

FIG. 20

FIG. 21

FIG. 22

FIG. 23

AN AMERICAN PANTRY

STORE-BOUGHT STAPLES

Condiments and pantry items organized by most frequently used.

FIG. 26

VINEGARS

BLACK VINEGAR — *FIG. 24*
Fruity, tangy, savory depth of flavor. I love using just a splash on savory dishes, along with a little soy sauce and a sprinkle of sugar. Black vinegar also works well alongside olive or grapeseed oil as a base for dressing. My go-to is always a bottle of Kong Yen Black Vinegar

RICE VINEGAR — *FIG. 25*

WHITE VINEGAR

BALSAMIC VINEGAR

APPLE CIDER VINEGAR

OILS

OLIVE OIL

GRAPESEED OIL
Great for infusing other ingredients, such as Scallion Oil (right)

VEGETABLE OIL
Neutral oil for pan-frying, my go-to for scallion pancakes or dumplings

SESAME OIL — *FIG. 26*
Fragrant nutty oil for adding flavor to dipping sauces, dumpling meat, and savory dishes

CHILI CRISP — *FIG. 27*
A vibrantly flavored oil infused with spices and crunchy aromatics. My go-to is Lao Gan Ma, the mother of all chili oils. I also love the flavors of Su Chili Crisp from Yun Hai Taiwanese Pantry and Fly By Jing's Sichuan Chili Crisp.

SAUCES AND SPREADS

SOY SAUCE
This book uses soy sauce in many recipes. My favorites include Wan Ja Shan Aged Soy Sauce and Amber River Soy Sauce from Yu Ding Xing Soy Sauce Brewery.

TIAN MIAN JIANG
A sweet umami sauce, eat me on noodles!

KETCHUP
Sweet tartness that mixes well with soy sauce, honey, and chili oils

MAYONNAISE
Perfect base for aiolis and dressings like the Cashew "Caesar" Salad (page 32)

MISO-FERMENTED SOYBEAN PASTE

HONEY

MAPLE SYRUP

ALMOND BUTTER

PEANUT BUTTER

ALCOHOL

SAKE — *FIG. 28*
Japanese rice wine

MIRIN — *FIG. 29*
Rice wine with sweetness, perfect for stir-fries and sauces

SHAOXING WINE
Chinese rice wine, adds depth to sauces, great marinade for meats as well

WHITE WINE

BULK

BROWN RICE

WHITE RICE — *FIG. 30*

SWEET GLUTINOUS RICE

SHIITAKE MUSHROOMS (DRIED)

KOMBU
Dried seaweed used for making dashi

FIG. 27

FLOURS

ALL-PURPOSE FLOUR

BREAD FLOUR

"00" FLOUR

GLUTINOUS RICE FLOUR

FIG. 28

FIG. 24

FIG. 29

FIG. 25

FIG. 30

HOMEMADE SAUCES, CONDIMENTS, AND STOCKS

The everyday dishes my family cooks are made simply. A bowl of white rice and scrambled eggs; leafy greens flash-fried in oil and garlic and then steamed in broth—these efficient preparations last mere minutes yet sustain us for multiple meals. Sauces, oils, and stocks can play a big part of adding flavor to these everyday dishes. Premade spoonfuls of aromatic oils can be tossed with plain noodles. A splash of sauce or stock can become the flavorful foundation to a sauté of vegetables. These homemade sauces, oils, and stocks are made to be versatile, drizzled and spread on whatever is being cooked to enhance flavor.

SAUCES AND CONDIMENTS

SCALLION OIL

This vibrant aromatic oil is made with fried scallions infused into grapeseed oil. I use it almost every day to add an additional level of fragrance and flavor to my food. It also works well as a base for dressings paired with black or balsamic vinegar or as a finishing oil drizzled on top of any savory dish that needs an aromatic boost, from scrambled eggs to roast vegetables.

MAKES ABOUT 2 CUPS

6 scallions, green and white parts, coarsely chopped
2 cups grapeseed oil

In a blender, combine the scallions and oil. Blend until completely smooth. Pour the mixture into a large skillet or pot and place over medium heat. Bring to a simmer and cook for 3 to 5 minutes, until fragrant and the scallion solids begin to separate from the oil. Remove from the heat and strain the oil through a fine-mesh strainer into a heatproof container. You should end up with a vibrantly green and transparent oil that's quite fragrant. Serve, or store in a sealed container in the fridge for up to 3 weeks.

SOY AND SCALLION SAUCE

Use as a base sauce to pour over simple steamed vegetables or cooked meats.

MAKES 1 CUP

1 tablespoon olive oil
3 scallions, green and white parts, chopped
1 teaspoon grated fresh ginger
½ cup water
3 teaspoons honey
2 tablespoons soy sauce
½ teaspoon white vinegar

In a small saucepan over medium heat, warm the oil. Add the scallions and ginger and sauté for 30 seconds, until fragrant. Reduce the heat to low and add the water, honey, soy sauce, and vinegar. Stir until incorporated. Serve, or store in a sealed container in the fridge for up to 4 days.

SPICY SOY AND SCALLION SAUCE

Use this sauce over any savory dishes, such as sautéed meats and vegetables or noodles and rice.

MAKES 1 CUP

1 tablespoon olive oil
½ teaspoon grated garlic
½ teaspoon grated fresh ginger
2 scallions, green and white parts, chopped
½ teaspoon white vinegar
2 tablespoons soy sauce
1 tablespoon chili crisp
¼ cup water
3 teaspoons maple syrup or honey
¼ teaspoon kosher salt

In a small saucepan over medium heat, warm the oil. Add the garlic, ginger, and scallions and sauté for 30 seconds, until fragrant. Reduce the heat to low and add the vinegar, soy sauce, chili crisp, water, maple syrup, and salt. Stir until incorporated. Serve, or cover and store in a sealed container in the fridge for up to 4 days.

ALMOND SOY GLAZE

This almond butter and soy–based sauce is reminiscent of the sweet-and-salty hoisin sauces used in the buns and scallion pancake wraps of my childhood. Use with fresh spring rolls, gua bao (an open-faced steamed bun typically filled with pork belly), noodles, or anything that needs bold depth of flavor.

MAKES 1¼ CUPS

¼ cup soy sauce
1 tablespoon water
3 tablespoons creamy almond butter
3 tablespoons maple syrup
1 teaspoon rice vinegar
2 teaspoons toasted sesame oil

In a small mixing bowl, combine the soy sauce, water, almond butter, maple syrup, vinegar, and sesame oil, and whisk until fully incorporated. Serve, or store in a sealed container in the fridge for up to 1 week.

PEANUT SAUCE

A versatile, classic peanut sauce with kicks of garlic and ginger. Use it as a base sauce for noodles, a dressing for salads, or a marinade for meat.

MAKES 1 CUP

1 teaspoon grated fresh ginger
1 teaspoon grated garlic
3 tablespoons creamy peanut butter
¼ cup warm water
2 tablespoons soy sauce
1 tablespoon honey
½ teaspoon kosher salt

In a small mixing bowl, combine the ginger, garlic, peanut butter, water, soy sauce, honey, and salt, and whisk until incorporated. Serve, or store in a sealed container in the fridge for up to 1 week.

SCALLION CASHEW CREAM

From the oozy Cheez Whiz on Ritz crackers to the spoonful of sour cream in Wendy's highly underrated chili, I gladly partake (with childlike enthusiasm) in any opportunity to top something with a cream or cheese in liquid form. This aromatic scallion cream is an ode to my love of cream and an homage to my lactose-intolerant ancestors (of which my family has many) by using cashews for the cream base. Use this as a rich topping for savory dishes that need that extra fattiness to finish.

MAKES 2 CUPS

2 cups raw unsalted cashews
¼ cup olive oil
8 scallions, green and white parts, cut into thirds
4 garlic cloves, smashed
3 teaspoons kosher salt
1 teaspoon granulated sugar
¼ teaspoon sweet paprika
Juice of ½ lemon
1 cup water

Place the cashews in a medium bowl; add cold water to cover by at least 1 inch and soak for at least 2 hours and up to overnight. Drain the cashews and set aside. In a medium saucepan over medium-high heat, warm the oil. Add the scallions and garlic; the oil should sizzle. Stir and cook for a few more minutes, until the scallions have softened slightly and the oil is fragrant. Transfer to a blender along with the soaked cashews, salt, sugar, paprika, lemon juice, and water. Blend until smooth, adjusting the salt or acid as needed. Serve, or store in a sealed container in the fridge for up to 1 week.

CHILI OIL KETCHUP

This versatile condiment made with ketchup and chili crisp has a spicy sweetness full of aromatic flavor from garlic and ginger. It's perfect for sandwiches, eggs, or anything that needs brightness.

MAKES 1½ CUPS

1 cup ketchup
2 tablespoons chili crisp
¼ cup maple syrup
1 teaspoon grated garlic
1 teaspoon grated fresh ginger
2 teaspoons soy sauce

In a blender, combine the ketchup, chili crisp, maple syrup, garlic, ginger, and soy sauce. Blend until smooth. Serve, or store in a sealed container in the fridge for up to 3 weeks.

STOCKS

CHICKEN STOCK

On its own, every sip of this simple chicken stock is nourishing. The hints of ginger and scallion layered throughout the subtle fattiness that comes from the chicken bones feel like a warm hug from Grandma. When used in other dishes, this chicken stock shows its true versatility as a base for building flavor and texture. In dumplings, a tablespoon of chicken stock helps create that ideal chewy-yet-light texture in the meat filling. In steamed egg (page 49), using this gelatin-rich chicken stock results in an incredibly silky custard. If using a whole chicken to create stock, you can pull the meat off to eat as well with rice. You can also use leftover bones or chicken carcasses from roasting as a base for this stock as well.

MAKES 3 QUARTS

One whole 4-pound chicken, broken down into breasts, drumsticks, thighs, and carcass, or 4 pounds chicken drumsticks or chicken bones
2 medium carrots, coarsely chopped
1 yellow onion, coarsely chopped
2 scallions, green and white parts, coarsely chopped
4 thumb-sized slices ginger
1 tablespoon kosher salt

Fill a large pot with cold water. Add the chicken pieces and bring to a boil. This method of blanching will bring the scum from the meat up to the surface, allowing for a cleaner, clearer broth.

Once scum from the chicken rises to the top, after about 10 minutes, drain the chicken and rinse it with hot water. Place the chicken back into the pot and add the carrots, onions, scallions, ginger, and salt. Pour in 3 quarts of cold water and bring to a boil. Reduce the heat to bring to a light simmer, with gentle bubbles breaking the surface. Cover and simmer for 3 hours, stirring occasionally. Taste the stock and season with more kosher salt if needed. Strain the stock by pouring it into a large fine-mesh metal sieve set over a large heatproof container. Store in a sealed container in the fridge for 3 to 4 days, or up to 3 months in the freezer.

PORK STOCK

Pork stock or pork bone soup is like water at our family's table. In fact, it replaced water and was our liquid of choice for hydration. Every meal I remember at home came with a light bowl of stock. Its natural lightness and clarity are a function of preboiling the meat beforehand to release all the impurities, which are then scooped out before slowly simmering the chicken with carrots and daikon. The resulting meat in this stock is delicious on its own, but I also love eating it with the Soy and Scallion Sauce (page 11) or just with salt and Scallion Oil (page 11). Serve or store in fridge for 4 days or up to 6 months in the freezer.

MAKES 3 QUARTS

3 pounds baby back pork or spare ribs, cut into pieces

2 tablespoons vegetable or olive oil

4 scallions, green and white parts, chopped

3 thumb-sized slices ginger

3 medium carrots, peeled and coarsely chopped

2 daikon, peeled and coarsely chopped

3 quarts cold water

Kosher salt

Fill a large pot with cold water. Add the pork and bring to a boil. Boil until the scum from the meat rises to the top, about 5 minutes. Fish out the pork with tongs and discard the water. Give the ribs a good rinse with hot water, then dry well with paper towels.

In a large saucepan over medium-high heat, warm the oil. Add the pork and lightly brown to seal in flavor. Place the browned pork into a large clean pot. Add the scallions, ginger, carrots, daikon, and water, and bring to a boil. Reduce the heat to bring to a light simmer, with gentle bubbles breaking the surface. Simmer for 3 to 4 hours, then turn the heat down low, cover, and simmer for 3 more hours, stirring occasionally. Taste the stock and season with salt to taste. Strain the stock by pouring it into a large fine-mesh metal sieve set over a large heatproof container. Store in a sealed container in the fridge for 3 to 4 days, or up to 3 months in the freezer.

SIMPLE VEGETABLE STOCK

This vegetable stock tastes like home. Napa cabbage, onion, and carrot slowly simmer and infuse this stock with a subtle sweetness that balances well with mushroom and scallions. Its flavors are simple yet nourishing, great on its own as a sipping broth or as a base to eat dumplings with or use for hot pot to simmer sliced meats and blanch leafy greens

MAKES 3 QUARTS

3 quarts cold water

½ medium head of napa cabbage, coarsely chopped

2 medium carrots, coarsely chopped

1 yellow onion, coarsely chopped

½ pound shiitake or oyster mushrooms, sliced

2 scallions, green and white parts, coarsely chopped

4 thumb-sized slices ginger

1 tablespoon kosher salt

Fill a large pot with the cold water. Add the cabbage, carrots, onions, mushrooms, scallions, ginger, and salt. Bring to a boil and then reduce the heat to a gentle simmer, with a light burp of bubbles just breaking the surface. Cover and simmer for 3 hours, stirring occasionally. Taste the stock and season with more salt if needed. Strain the stock by pouring it into a large fine-mesh metal sieve set over a large heatproof container. Store in a sealed container in the fridge for 3 to 4 days, or up to 3 months in the freezer.

HANGOVER CHICKEN AND VEGETABLE SOUP

Here's a chicken-and-vegetable soup made to be chunky, warm, and sustaining in moments that require comfort after a long night out or a stressful day. It's one of those dishes that wasn't necessarily meant to be a recipe. The soul of this dish comes from pulling what's left over in the fridge—an odd knob of ginger here, a half head of cabbage there—and bringing them together in one pot. Serve as is or mix in cooked rice and fresh greens.

MAKES 3 QUARTS

2 tablespoons unsalted butter

2 sweet onions, diced

6 to 8 garlic cloves, smashed

10 thumb-sized slices ginger

3 to 4 pounds boneless, skinless chicken thighs, cut into small chunks

4 medium carrots, peeled and coarsely chopped

1 small daikon, peeled and coarsely chopped

2 ears corn, husked and cut in half

½ small napa cabbage, cored and separated into leaves

3 quarts cold water

2 tablespoons mirin

2 tablespoons kosher salt

1 tablespoon rice vinegar

Cooked white rice (optional)

Fresh leafy greens (optional)

In a large pot over low-medium heat, melt the butter. Add the onions, garlic, and ginger, cook, stirring occasionally, until the onions have softened, about 10 minutes.

Add the chicken, carrots, daikon, corn, and cabbage to the pot. Add the water, mirin, and salt. Bring to a boil, then lower to a gentle simmer and cook uncovered for 2 hours. Add the rice vinegar, then taste. Add more salt or vinegar if needed. To serve, ladle into individual bowls and add a spoonful of cooked white rice and some leafy greens, if using. Serve, or store in a sealed container in the fridge for up to 5 days.

SM

IALL EATS

Steven

"Steven?" my grandma asks.

"Hi, Grandma—no, it's me, Frankie. Steven is your oldest grandson."

We're sitting at my grandma's table in her small, cozy kitchen in Memphis, during our annual Thanksgiving visit. The table, as always, is filled with small eats: A plastic container of never-ending peanuts that have been marinated in soy sauce and roasted. Open plastic bags of crunchy rice crackers with their glossy surface of soy glaze. Peeled clementines resting on a paper napkin.

"You don't look like Frankie," my grandma replies as she delicately reaches for a peanut. "How old are you?"

"I'm twenty-nine years old, Grandma."

"Twenty-nine?! That can't be." I see her pause, her thoughts swimming within the depths of her cognition. Her brain reaching for the surface that is her memory only to be swallowed deep into the past. To her, Frankie is her youngest grandson, a child, not this adult looming before her.

"Yes, twenty-nine!"

"You should have a bride by now!" she exclaims. "Are you married yet?"

"Not yet, Grandma," I reply.

"I know some eligible ladies," she says with a smile. "I can introduce them to you. They live down the street from us in Taipei, all very pretty."

"That sounds great, Grandma." I've eaten half the container of peanuts without even realizing.

"Steven?"

"Hi, Grandma. It's Frankie."

"Frankie?"

"Yes, your youngest grandson. Do you remember?"

"Yes, I do remember. You look like Steven."

I sigh. "I'm just older now since you've last seen me. I'm almost thirty years old!"

"Wow!" she exclaims. "Are you married yet?"

I turn to my mom, my raised eyebrows expressing what I can't say out loud as I think of my boyfriend back home. My mom, who has an uncanny ability to read my thoughts, responds with a glare that insists *now is not the time*.

"Actually, yes, Grandma, I am!"

Her face lights up.

"In fact, I have eighteen wives."

"Eighteen?!?!" My grandma lets out the biggest belly laugh. For someone so fragile, her laugh is a guttural response that comes from the belly, requiring the core strength of someone much younger as she grips her wheelchair and throws her head back, her eyes closed as she howls in pure enjoyment.

It always makes me smile.

"Yes, eighteen! I did quite well."

"You sure did!"

"Steven?"

"Hi, Grandma. How are you today?"

"I'm good. Are you Steven?"

"No, it's Frankie, Grandma."

"Ah, okay. Frankie then. You look much older, when are you getting married?"

There's so much I wish I could tell her.

"One day, Grandma. One day."

I grab a sliced half of hard-boiled egg that's been marinated in soy sauce, its yolk orange like a sunset captured in a deep brown. A dish that has been a consistent companion at my grandma's kitchen table for as long as I can remember.

"Grandma, will you teach me how to make this one day?"

"Yes, of course. We can go to the market later today to get the ingredients.

We can make soy-marinated eggs, steamed bao. . . . I'll make many dishes for dinner tonight."

My grandma has been bound to a wheelchair for a few years now, where her body and mind have both been trapped. But even as her mind struggles with the present, her memory flourishes in the past. She'll describe how we'll go to the Chinese market, where she'll pick out the right cut of pork shoulder. She tells me her plans for how she'll make me the silkiest dan bing (Taiwanese egg crepes) for me in the morning like she has since I was five. She'll walk me through dinner prep: finely dice Chinese chives to mix with rice noodles for chive pockets; hand mix pork, ginger, and scallion until the fat binds with the meat and is perfectly sticky; knead dough five hundred times until it's bouncy for that perfect QQ (a Taiwanese term loosely translated to "al dente" or "perfectly chewy") texture. I capture glimmers of recipes as she speaks, faint wisps of her vast breadth of knowledge, holding onto everything in my memory for as long as possible. It's an ensemble of ingredients and dishes of my childhood for a feast that she'll forget within the half hour.

"Steven?"

"Hi Grandma, it's me, your youngest grandson, Frankie."

"Frankie." She pauses. "Where's your father? 金濤? Is he here?"

I place my chopsticks down near my plate of sliced cucumbers. I don't hear my dad's name very often. It only comes up when I hear my grandma ask for her son year after year. I want to cry but I physically cannot. Not because I'm choosing not to but because my mom is too scared that the emotion will give away the reality of my dad's whereabouts. The answer would literally give my grandma a heart attack. I give the same response from years past.

"He's on a business trip to China," I reply.

"How is he doing?" she asks. "I haven't seen him in a long time."

I nervously pick at the cucumbers in front of me, the slices soaking in a glistening pool of acidity from salt and rice vinegar.

"He's doing good, working very hard, always traveling. He'll be back to see you soon."

My grandma continues to eat and I instinctually go to the bathroom. I turn the fan on and pull a sweater over my head to muffle any sound as I let everything out.

Back at the table, my grandma's eyes meet mine.

"Frankie."

"Grandma! Yes! Hi! It's me!"

I scoot my chair closer to her. "You can tell it's me?"

"Hah!" she yells. "Really? How could I not recognize my youngest grandson?!"

I hold my grandma's delicate hand, its fragility a mirage for what it's truly capable of in the kitchen.

"Grandma, you know I love you, right?"

Her attention is back to the small eats, the roasted peanuts.

"I love you too," she says.

"Well, I love you too," I reply with more enthusiasm.

"I LOVE YOU!" she yells back at me.

"I LOVE YOU!!!!" I scream back in her face.

We're both belly laughing now.

BRAISED PEANUTS

If my family had a mascot, it would probably be a peanut. My memory is filled with them: My dad's Costco-size order of Planters Honey Roasted Peanuts, always a spoon's length away from any dish. My grandma's endless bowl of soy-marinated peanuts, leaving a coat of grease on my iPhone the rest of the day because I couldn't stop eating them. One of my favorite iterations of the peanut is the braised peanut. In this recipe, garlic, scallions, and chili flakes bathe peanuts in an aromatic oil Jacuzzi. Texturally, these peanuts sit between a peanut and a bean, perfectly al dente from their soak in olive oil and black vinegar. They're a delightful table snack.

3 cups raw unsalted peanuts, shelled

½ cup olive oil or grapeseed oil

3 scallions, green and white parts, finely chopped, plus more for garnish

2 garlic cloves, sliced

1 teaspoon red pepper flakes

2 tablespoons black vinegar or rice vinegar

3 teaspoons kosher salt

2 teaspoons granulated sugar

Cilantro leaves for garnish

Makes 2 servings

Place the peanuts in a medium bowl; add cold water to cover by at least 1 inch. Soak at room temperature at least 2 hours or up to overnight. Drain the peanuts and lightly pat them dry. In a large saucepan over medium heat, warm the oil. Add the scallions, garlic, and red pepper flakes, and fry until sizzling and fragrant, 2 to 3 minutes. Add the drained peanuts to the pan and stir, coating them with the seasoned oil and aromatics. Add the vinegar, salt, and sugar and continue to mix until fully incorporated. Pour the peanuts into a serving bowl and let them marinate for 10 minutes, then top with scallions and cilantro and serve. Store any leftovers in the fridge for up to 1 week.

19

Dried soybeans are boiled, pureed, and strained to create this classic creamy drink. My undeniable sweet tooth loves this soy milk warmed and sweetened with some honey.

SOY MILK

Bring a large pot of water to a boil over high heat. Add the soybeans and boil for 10 minutes, until softened. Drain and transfer to a blender. Add the 8 cups water and blend until smooth, about 30 seconds on a high-speed blender. (You may have to do this in two batches depending on the size of your blender.) Strain the mixture through cheesecloth or a nut milk bag, then pour the strained soy milk back into the large pot and bring to a simmer. Simmer for 20 minutes, stirring constantly so it doesn't boil or burn on the bottom of the pot. Let cool, then pour into a container with a lid and store in the fridge for up to 5 days.

2 cups dried organic soybeans

8 cups water

Makes 2 quarts

COLD MARINATED PICKLES

Here's a side dish that's easily overlooked—not because it's a simple dish of sliced cucumbers typically eaten from a plastic Tupperware. No, it's easily overlooked because when that plastic Tupperware is placed on a kitchen island, those cucumber slices glistening from their soak in salt, sugar, and rice vinegar get consumed so fast that by the time the rest of the family gathers in the kitchen, cucumbers are nowhere to be found. This simple pickle is a staple of many a kitchen island. Its versatility lies in its method, where salt flavors the cucumber while pulling out excess moisture, allowing the cucumber to soak in the flavors from the sugar, vinegar, and the chili oil. Persian cucumbers typically work best with this recipe but if you can't find Persian, English cucumbers work as a fine substitute.

1 pound Persian cucumbers (6 to 8), sliced ½ inch thick

3 tablespoons light brown sugar

2 tablespoons kosher salt

4 garlic cloves, thinly sliced

1 tablespoon toasted sesame oil

1 tablespoon chili crisp (optional)

2 teaspoons rice vinegar or lemon juice

sesame seeds

Makes 3 servings

In a medium mixing bowl, combine the cucumbers, brown sugar, and salt, and gently use your hands to massage the sugar and salt into the cucumbers until evenly coated. Place the bowl in the fridge and let the cucumbers marinate for at least 30 minutes and up to a few hours to absorb the seasoning and release water. While the cucumbers marinate, in a small bowl, combine the garlic, sesame oil, chili crisp (if using), and vinegar, and whisk to combine. Set aside. Once the cucumbers are marinated, drain to remove excess water, and return to the mixing bowl. Pour the dressing onto the cucumbers, toss to combine, and serve with a sprinkle of sesame seeds. Store covered in the fridge for up to 5 days.

SOFT-BOILED TEA EGGS

Eggs marinated in tea leaves and soy make a snack that has become ubiquitous in kitchens and 7-Eleven convenience stores across Taiwan. This version features a soft-boiled, slightly oozy center that's simmered in a comforting blend of oolong tea, soy sauce, and aromatics that will fill your kitchen with fragrance.

4 cups water

¾ cup soy sauce

2 thumb-sized slices ginger

3 garlic cloves, peeled

2 tablespoons oolong tea leaves

2 bay leaves

1 star anise pod

1 cinnamon stick

1 tablespoon kosher salt

1 tablespoon light brown sugar

8 eggs

Makes 4 servings

In a large pot, combine the water, soy sauce, ginger, garlic, tea, bay leaves, star anise, cinnamon, salt, and brown sugar, and bring to a boil. Reduce the heat and simmer for 15 to 20 minutes, until fragrant. With a slotted spoon or strainer, gently lower the eggs into the pot. Cook for 6 minutes and 30 seconds. While the eggs cook, prepare an ice bath in a large bowl. With the spoon or strainer, remove the eggs and place them in the ice bath. Pour the brine into a heatproof container and let cool. Once the brine is cool, peel the eggs and place them in the container, cover, and marinate overnight. Serve the following day or store in the fridge for up to 2 days.

I'm a former broccoli hater. Broccoli's only true redeeming quality in my early life was its role as an edible utensil, its presence on a black plastic Costco tray of raw vegetables a mere audience to the true star: the rich, creamy dips at the center. Since then, I've come to love all things broccoli, including its friends broccolini and Chinese broccoli, typically enhancing their flavor with a blanching in boiling water or a caramelizing in the oven. This dish uses broccolini (a cross between broccoli and Chinese broccoli), but regular broccoli or Chinese broccoli can easily be used as substitutes. The broccolini gets roasted in the oven for a little char, and is then tossed with Persian cucumbers that have been marinated in chili crisp and toasted sesame oil to take on acidity and nuttiness. The salad has its final resting place on a spread of luscious scallion cashew cream, topped with crunchy peanuts and a spritz of lemon.

CHARRED BROCCOLINI AND CUCUMBER SALAD WITH SCALLION CASHEW CREAM

BRINE THE CUCUMBERS: In a medium mixing bowl, combine the cucumber slices, sugar, and salt. Use your hands to massage the sugar and salt into the cucumbers until evenly coated. Let the cucumbers marinate for at least 30 minutes and up to a few hours in the fridge to absorb the seasoning and release water.

MAKE THE BROCCOLINI: Preheat the oven to 425°F. Trim off the bottom quarter of the broccolini stems. Cut any large stems in half lengthwise. On a large baking sheet, toss the broccolini with a generous amount of olive oil and sprinkle with salt and pepper. Give the broccolini a nice olive oil massage with your hands, making sure it's coated evenly. Spread out in an even layer on the baking sheet and roast for 20 minutes, until slightly charred and cooked through. Transfer to a large mixing bowl and set aside.

MAKE THE DRESSING: In a small mixing bowl, combine the sesame oil, chili crisp, and garlic, and mix to incorporate.

Once the cucumbers are marinated, pour out the excess water and pour the dressing onto the cucumbers. Toss to mix. Add the dressed cucumbers to the mixing bowl with the broccolini and give it a good toss. To serve, spoon a generous amount of scallion cashew cream on the bottom of a plate. Place the broccolini and cucumbers on top. Top with chopped scallions and peanuts and a sprinkle of lemon juice and lemon zest, and serve.

CUCUMBERS

1 pound Persian cucumbers (6 to 8), sliced ½ inch thick

3 tablespoons granulated sugar or light brown sugar

2 tablespoons kosher salt

BROCCOLINI

1 bunch broccolini (12 ounces)

Olive oil

Kosher salt and freshly ground black pepper

DRESSING

1 tablespoon toasted sesame oil

1 tablespoon chili crisp

4 garlic cloves, thinly sliced

TOPPINGS

Scallion Cashew Cream (page 12)

Chopped scallions

Chopped peanuts

Lemon juice and zest

Makes 3 servings

I used to hate carrots. Mostly because my mom gave them to me raw on salads and told me I had to eat them or I'd go blind. But at age twenty-three, at Zuni Café in San Francisco, a dish of roasted carrots, with their slightly burnt skin and sweet inner texture, carried me from intense carrot distaste to caramelized vegetable bliss. A rotation of 5-pound bags of whole carrots has never left my refrigerator's sight since. A simple roasted carrot with salt, pepper, and olive oil typically satisfies when I'm lazy, but when I want to treat myself, the extra effort to add some depth through acid and fresh herbs does make it quite special. With black vinegar and soy sauce along with rosemary and olive oil, I'd like to think this dish was conceived by my grandma while hanging out with Samin Nosrat in her Berkeley kitchen. Both are drinking glasses of red wine while eating the carrots right from the baking sheet with their fingers. Carrot bliss indeed.

ROASTED CARROTS WITH ROSEMARY, GARLIC, AND BLACK VINEGAR

Preheat the oven to 425°F. Cut any large carrots in half lengthwise, while leaving small-to-medium carrots whole. Place on a baking sheet and coat generously with olive oil, then season with salt and pepper and use your hands to massage everything together. Cook for 30 minutes, until tender, flipping the carrots halfway through to evenly brown them.

While the carrots are cooking, in a small mixing bowl, combine the black vinegar, soy sauce, sesame oil, scallion oil, brown sugar, garlic, ginger, and rosemary and stir well to incorporate. Set aside.

When the carrots are done roasting (if they can be easily pierced with a knife, they're done), cover them evenly with the black vinegar marinade and let sit for 10 minutes. Place the carrots on a serving plate, garnish with scallions, sesame seeds, scallion cashew cream (if using), and more salt to taste, and serve.

2 pounds carrots, peeled and trimmed

Olive oil

Kosher salt and freshly ground black pepper

2 tablespoons black vinegar

1½ tablespoons soy sauce

½ teaspoon toasted sesame oil

2 tablespoons Scallion Oil (page 11) or olive oil

1 tablespoon light brown sugar

1 garlic clove, grated

1 teaspoon grated fresh ginger

1 teaspoon finely chopped fresh rosemary

Chopped scallions for garnish

Sesame seeds for garnish

Scallion Cashew Cream (page 12), optional, for garnish

Makes 2 servings

LAP CHEONG
CORN DOGS

It starts with a love of Costco corn dogs, a daily ritual of microwaving and savoring their salty sweetness with a dab of ketchup after school. It's paired with a craving for distinctly sweet Chinese sausages, always the best surprise at the center of a zongzi (glutinous sticky rice stuffed with a meat filling) or in a spoonful of fried rice. It's a tale of two ingredients from different worlds, yet a dream pairing of cornbread batter and Chinese sausage—destined to be together in the mind of a young Asian American kid from suburban Ohio.

14-ounce package lap cheong Chinese sausages (about 10)

1 cup cornmeal

1 cup all-purpose flour

2 teaspoons baking powder

2 teaspoons kosher salt

½ cup plain Greek yogurt

2 eggs

⅔ cup unsweetened almond milk

¼ cup plus 2 tablespoons maple syrup

Vegetable oil or canola oil for frying

Chili Oil Ketchup (page 12) for serving

Scallion Cashew Cream (page 12) for serving

Makes 10 corn dogs

Bring a large pot of water to a boil. Add the lap cheong and boil for 15 minutes (or cook according to package instructions). Meanwhile, in a large mixing bowl, combine the cornmeal, flour, baking powder, and salt and whisk until smooth. In a medium mixing bowl, whisk the yogurt, eggs, almond milk, and maple syrup until combined. Pour the wet ingredients into the dry ingredients and stir together to create the corn dog batter. Pour the batter into a skinny glass, taller than the sausage is long.

Once the sausages are cooked through, rinse them in cold water to cool down. Skewer each sausage with a wooden skewer, starting from the bottom and pushing through until it reaches three-quarters of the way up.

Set out a wire cooling rack, or cover a work surface with paper towels. Pour the vegetable oil into a large pot to a depth of 4 inches and warm over medium heat until the oil reaches 375°F. (Use a deep-fry thermometer to check the temperature. If you don't have a thermometer, use a chopstick: the oil is ready when a light simmering of bubbles rises to the top when you dip the chopstick into the oil. If the bubbles are aggressive like a Jacuzzi jet, turn the heat down to reduce the temperature.)

Once the oil has reached frying temperature, dunk a sausage straight into the glass of batter, submerging it completely. Give it a spin in the batter to coat evenly, then pull it back up. With tongs gripping the end of a skewer, very carefully place the corn dog into the oil and fry until the batter has become a light golden brown, turning as needed to brown evenly, 3 to 4 minutes. Remove the corn dog from the oil and place onto the rack or paper towels to cool. Repeat with the remaining skewered sausages. Serve immediately, with a drizzle of chili ketchup and scallion cream.

WARM SWEET POTATO AND ZUCCHINI SHREDDED SALAD

This recipe is a simple homestyle dish by my grandma. Though she typically uses white potatoes, in my version, sweet potato makes a cameo appearance; it's julienned and soaked in water and vinegar, which removes excess sugar and starch to create its signature crisp texture. Garlic, scallions, and red pepper flakes sizzling in a pool of oil coat each individual slice of sweet potato and zucchini with aromatic heat as it cooks through to completion. My grandma loves riffing on this recipe, swapping out different types of potatoes or adding complementary vegetables. Any vegetable you can julienne—think bell peppers, celery, or carrots—are all part of the joy of experiencing this recipe's possibilities. Serve warm or refrigerate overnight and enjoy as a cold salad.

1 medium sweet potato

2 tablespoons rice vinegar or white vinegar

1 medium zucchini

2 tablespoons vegetable oil

2 garlic cloves, sliced

1/2 teaspoon red pepper flakes

2 scallions, green and white parts, chopped, plus more for garnish

1/2 teaspoon light brown sugar

Kosher salt

White sesame seeds

Makes 2 servings

PREP THE VEGETABLES: Cut the sweet potato at an angle into 1/8-inch-thick slices to get oval disks. Stack a few slices at a time and slice into 1/8-inch-thick sticks until all the sweet potato has been used. Put the sweet potato sticks in a bowl filled with water and 1 tablespoon of the vinegar and let soak for 10 minutes. While the potato is soaking, cut the zucchini at a diagonal into thin ovals, stack the ovals, and slice to get thin sticks the same size as the sweet potato sticks. Set aside.

STIR-FRY: In a large skillet or pot over medium heat, warm the oil. Add the garlic, red pepper flakes, and scallions. Cook, stirring, until fragrant, a couple minutes or so.

Drain the sweet potato and add to the skillet. Cook for a few minutes, until the potatoes have just slightly softened, then add the zucchini sticks and continue to stir to cook evenly.

Add the remaining 1 tablespoon vinegar and the brown sugar to the skillet and stir to combine. Cook for a couple more minutes, until the potatoes have softened but still have bite and the zucchini is tender. Turn the heat off and add salt to taste. Serve topped with sesame seeds and chopped scallions.

SHREDDED SALADS

Shredded salads are very versatile—just use the recipe at left and mix and match different ingredients as well as toppings.

Celery, celery leaves, potato, chives

Bell pepper, potato, scallions

Potato, sesame seeds, scallions

Carrot, potato, scallions, broccoli stems

CASHEW "CAESAR" SALAD

This is an ode to my mom's "Caesar salads." They weren't very good, to be honest. In fact, salads traumatized me my entire childhood, an unwelcome surprise lurking on the table when all I wanted to eat were cookies. This is the version of my mom's salad I wish I'd had, without the bottles of Hidden Valley and heaps of raw carrots and broccoli that she insisted I eat for my growth spurt that never happened. Crisp romaine hearts are tossed in a cashew-based Caesar dressing blended with anchovies, garlic, and mayonnaise. Grated Parmesan paired with spicy chili crisp and chopped scallions makes this salad a tribute to my grandma's pantry and my mom's valiant efforts.

DRESSING

⅓ cup roasted unsalted cashews

2 garlic cloves, minced

1 anchovy fillet, chopped (½ teaspoon)

1 teaspoon light brown sugar

1 teaspoon kosher salt

¼ cup olive oil

1 tablespoon lemon juice

¼ cup mayonnaise

GREENS

1 head romaine lettuce

TOPPINGS

Black or white sesame seeds

Chopped scallions

Chili crisp

Grated Parmesan cheese

Kosher salt and freshly ground black pepper

Makes 4 servings

MAKE THE DRESSING: In a mortar and pestle or food processor, grind or blend the cashews, garlic, anchovy, brown sugar, and salt into a rough paste. Add the oil a tablespoon at a time and continue grinding or blending until it becomes a smoother, thick paste. Transfer the paste to a small mixing bowl and add the lemon juice and mayonnaise. Whisk until smooth.

MIX THE SALAD: Separate the lettuce into individual leaves. Place the lettuce in a large mixing bowl. Spoon the dressing onto the lettuce and mix with your hands to coat evenly. Put the dressed greens on a serving plate and sprinkle with the sesame seeds and scallions. Top with a drizzle of chili crisp and a snowy pile of grated Parmesan cheese. Add salt and pepper to taste, and serve.

ARUGULA AND KALE SALAD WITH BALSAMIC MISO SCALLION VINAIGRETTE

If you ever find yourself in San Francisco, I'd encourage you to gather your friends and attend trivia night at Hi Tops in the Castro, a gay sports bar in my old stomping grounds. Not only are the trivia team names worthy of a visit alone, but the food is also spectacular. Their iconic kale salad is anything but simple; they mix fresh kale and crispy roasted kale chips for an extra dimension of crunch and salt. My version is an homage to Hi Tops and the Castro—I use arugula and kale chips to create that same satisfying crunch. The dressing here is the highlight, an emulsion of tart balsamic and miso umami with scallion oil as its base. A final touch of shredded Parmesan and chopped scallions creates a salad that brings Hi Tops and my kitchen to your home.

SALAD

1 bunch lacinato kale, ribs removed

1 tablespoon olive oil

½ pound arugula

DRESSING

4 teaspoons balsamic vinegar

2 tablespoons white miso

4 teaspoons honey

½ cup Scallion Oil (page 11), plus more for garnish

TOPPINGS

Shredded Parmesan cheese

Chopped scallions

Makes 4 servings

MAKE THE KALE CHIPS: Preheat the oven to 275°F. Place half the kale leaves on a baking sheet in a single layer. Drizzle with olive oil and toss with your hands to evenly coat the leaves. Bake for 20 minutes, flipping halfway through, until the kale is crispy and brittle. Remove from the oven and set aside.

MAKE THE DRESSING: In a small mixing bowl, whisk together the balsamic vinegar, miso, honey, and scallion oil until smooth and emulsified.

ASSEMBLE THE SALAD: Chop the remaining raw kale into bite-sized pieces and place in a large mixing bowl. Add the arugula and the roasted kale chips. Pour the dressing over and mix with your hands until fully incorporated. Top with a flurry of Parmesan cheese, a sprinkling of chopped scallions, and a drizzle of scallion oil, and serve.

A vegetable for the non–vegetable lovers in the world, corn has a special place in my heart. Corn reminds me of my dad, who used to buy cans of corn in bulk and blend them together into a simple soup that fueled my childhood. Sometimes it would be chunky like a stew—a simple pot of water filled with kernels of corn, salt, and an egg swirled into the soup as it was cooking. Other times, he would blend all the ingredients together, similar to a Japanese corn potage like the recipe here. This soup is simple in nature, just corn and aromatics getting to know each other in a pot of water, then blended and strained for a creamy spoonful of comfort.

CREAMY CORN SOUP

Kernels from
3 ears of corn,
cobs reserved

1 tablespoon
olive oil

1/4 teaspoon sweet
paprika

Kosher salt and
freshly ground
black pepper

1/2 tablespoon
unsalted butter

1 sweet onion,
coarsely chopped

Chopped cilantro
for garnish

Makes 4 to 6 servings

ROAST THE CORN: Preheat the oven to 400°F and line a baking sheet with parchment paper. Place the corn kernels on the baking sheet and toss with the oil, paprika, and a sprinkle each of salt and pepper. Roast for 8 minutes, until the kitchen smells like popcorn. Remove from the oven and set aside.

COOK THE ONION AND CORN: In a large pot over medium heat, melt the butter. Add the onion and cook until semitranslucent and softened, stirring frequently to evenly cook. Pour the roasted corn kernels into the pot. Stir for a minute or so to let the corn and onions mingle.

SIMMER THE SOUP: Add water to the pot until it's about an inch or two above the ingredients. Submerge the reserved corn cobs in the pot of water (they will give an extra boost of corn flavor to the soup). Bring the mixture to a boil, then let it hang out at a low simmer for 15 to 20 minutes to let the flavors meld together. Taste the broth periodically for the desired amount of saltiness and add salt to taste.

BLEND THE SOUP: After the soup has finished simmering, remove and discard the cobs and pour the contents of the pot into a blender. Blend until completely smooth, adding salt or pepper as needed. Serve the corn soup as is, or pour through a fine-mesh metal sieve to achieve a completely smooth texture.

Pour the soup into bowls and top with cilantro to serve. Store in a sealed container in the fridge for up to a few days or in the freezer for up to 3 months.

Tip:
To make this into a corn–and–egg drop soup, blend the soup as directed in the recipe. Return the soup to the pot and heat to a low simmer. In a small mixing bowl, whisk together 2 eggs, then stir the pot vigorously to create a whirlpool. As the soup spins around, slowly drizzle in the beaten eggs to create ribbons of texture. Serve, garnished with the cilantro.

GRANDMA'S PEARL MEATBALLS

This was one of the very first recipes my grandma taught me when I started learning to cook from her. I had never even seen it before she taught me. I remember following her lead as she combined a familiar mixture of pork, ginger, and scallions into a meatball, then rolled it in grains of sweet glutinous rice that looked like pearls. After an 18-minute steam, lifting the steamer lid revealed glistening sticky rice balls, every grain soaked with pork juice and the aroma of bamboo. I can trace this recipe back to the Hubei province of China; it's one of the dishes that makes me proud to be Asian. Though it's simple, with minimal ingredients, it delivers so much soul. When steaming these meatballs, I find it best to line a bamboo steamer with liners that are perforated or with extra napa cabbage leaves.

RICE
1 cup sweet glutinous rice

FILLING
½ medium head (1 pound) napa cabbage, finely minced

1 tablespoon plus ½ teaspoon kosher salt

1 pound ground pork or freshly ground pork shoulder

1 tablespoon minced garlic (3 cloves)

1 teaspoon minced fresh ginger

3 scallions, green and white parts, chopped

2 teaspoons light brown sugar

2 teaspoons toasted sesame oil

1 tablespoon chicken stock

Vegetable oil, for forming the meatballs

Makes 24 meatballs

SOAK THE RICE: The night before, place the glutinous rice in a medium mixing bowl. Add water to cover by 1 inch and place in the fridge to soak overnight.

MAKE THE FILLING: In a large mixing bowl, combine the cabbage and the ½ teaspoon salt. Mix with your fingers until the salt is incorporated. Set aside for 10 minutes to let the cabbage sweat out water. Meanwhile, in another large bowl, combine the ground pork, garlic, ginger, scallions, brown sugar, sesame oil, the remaining 1 tablespoon salt, and the chicken stock.

After the cabbage has sweated out all its water, transfer it onto a thin dish towel or a few layers of thick paper towels and wrap around the cabbage to enclose. Using your hands and brute strength, squeeze out as much excess water from the cabbage as you can. Transfer the cabbage to the rest of the filling mixture and use your fingers to mix all that juicy meat-mixture goodness together, using a circular motion, until the filling looks homogeneous and feels sticky, about 3 minutes.

MAKE THE MEATBALLS: Drain the rice, then pour the grains onto a plate. Prep a bamboo steamer by lining it with perforated steamer liners or extra napa cabbage leaves. With oiled hands, grab a small amount of meat filling (the size of a ping-pong ball) and roll it into a meatball. Then roll the meatball around in the plate of rice until the grains have stuck to the entire surface of the meatball. Set the meatball into the bamboo steamer. Continue forming meatballs and rolling them in rice until all the meat filling has been used.

STEAM THE MEATBALLS: Fill a pot that will fit your bamboo steamer with an inch of water and bring to a boil. Place the steamer in the pot and cover. Steam for 18 minutes, until the rice has softened and the meat is cooked through, and serve.

Bread. The fourth love of my life after dumplings, french fries, and cookies. Clearly my life choices are run by carbs. I'm just a simple boy raised on processed white Wonder Bread and sustained by trips to Cracker Barrel for cornbread. The flavors of this recipe are a combination of these two memories, while texturally it leans closer to the fluffy milk breads I ate from the Asian markets of my childhood. The final act of this bread is when it's made into Maple Toast (page 203), where it's smothered with maple butter and topped with flaky salt and black sesame seeds. See pages 40–41 for step-by-step illustrations for making this bread.

MAKE THE CORNMEAL MIXTURE: In a medium saucepan over medium heat, combine the cornmeal, brown sugar, salt, butter, and almond milk. Stir together until the mixture has thickened into a gloopy paste. Transfer to a large mixing bowl and set aside to cool.

MAKE THE DOUGH AND PROOF: In a small mixing bowl, combine the yeast and the 1/4 teaspoon granulated sugar. Mix in the warm almond milk to activate the yeast, and let the mixture sit for 5 minutes, until it foams. While the yeast is activating, to the large bowl with the cornmeal mixture, add the remaining 2 tablespoons granulated sugar, bread flour, egg, and salt. Add in the activated yeast mixture. Mix everything together with a rubber spatula or stand mixer until the ingredients are incorporated and a rough dough ball starts to take shape. Transfer the dough to a clean work surface and knead for 5 to 10 minutes, until smooth (if it's sticky, dust with a little bit of extra flour or oil your hands). Place the dough in a clean, large mixing bowl and cover with plastic wrap. Proof for 1 hour in a warm, draft-free place until it has doubled in size.

SHAPE AND DO A SECOND PROOF: Punch the dough down and divide it into 3 equal pieces. Shape each piece into a smooth ball, then place on a plate or cutting board. Cover the dough with plastic wrap and let it rest for 15 minutes.

Uncover and roll each ball into a thick oval the size of your hand. Fold the oval into thirds crosswise to create a rectangle. With the shorter end facing you, roll the rectangle into a fat burrito and pinch the seam at the end to seal. Repeat with the rest of the dough pieces.

Oil the bottom and sides of a loaf pan (approximately 8.5 by 4.75 inches). Place the dough pieces next to each other in the loaf pan, seam sides down. Lightly brush the top of the dough with water and dust with cornmeal. Cover the loaf pan with plastic wrap and proof in a warm, draft-free place for 1 hour, until the dough has doubled in size.

When the dough is almost proofed, preheat the oven to 375°F. Remove the plastic wrap and bake for 30 minutes, until the crust is golden brown. Carefully pop the bread out of the loaf pan and cool on a wire rack. Slice to serve.

FLUFFY CORNMEAL WHITE BREAD

CORNMEAL MIXTURE

1/2 cup cornmeal

1/4 cup light brown sugar

1/2 teaspoon kosher salt

4 tablespoons unsalted butter

1 cup almond milk

DOUGH MIXTURE

1 tablespoon active dry yeast

2 tablespoons plus 1/4 teaspoon granulated sugar

3/4 cup almond milk, heated to 110° to 120°F

2 3/4 cups bread flour

1 egg

1 tablespoon kosher salt

TOPPING

Cornmeal for dusting

Makes 1 loaf

FLUFFY CORNMEAL WHITE BREAD

1.

Mix together in a pan over medium heat *Mix until it's thick and gloopy*

2.

Mix, then wait 5 minutes until it foams *Mix everything together*

3.

Knead until smooth, 5 to 10 minutes *Cover and proof*

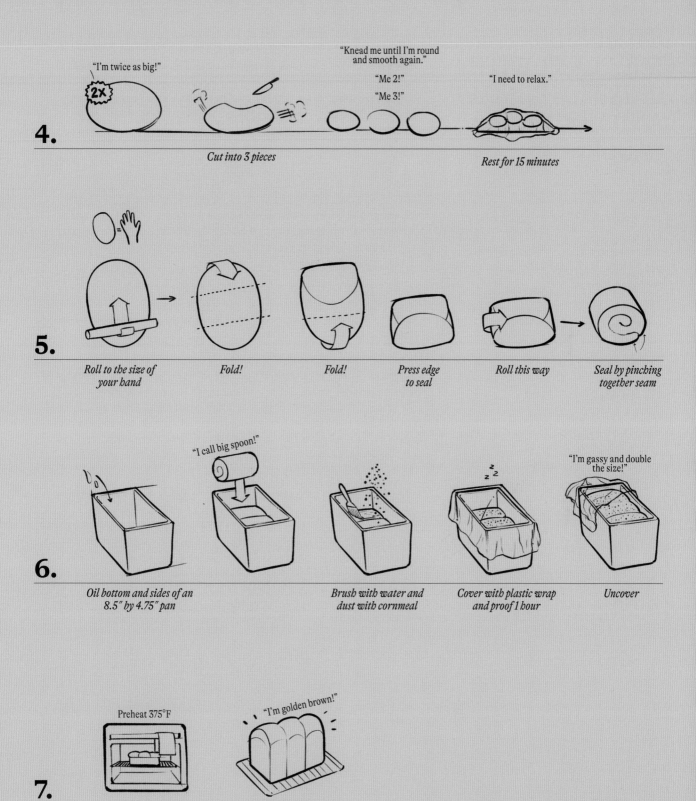

4. Cut into 3 pieces — Rest for 15 minutes

5. Roll to the size of your hand — Fold! — Fold! — Press edge to seal — Roll this way — Seal by pinching together seam

6. Oil bottom and sides of an 8.5" by 4.75" pan — Brush with water and dust with cornmeal — Cover with plastic wrap and proof 1 hour — Uncover

7. Bake 30 minutes — Cool on wire rack

STEAMED EGGPLANT WITH CRISPED QUINOA AND MIRIN MISO SAUCE

I love this classic Taiwanese homestyle preparation—vegetables simply steamed till they're just cooked through. A little trick I learned from my family is to soak the eggplant slices in water and vinegar, which helps the eggplant keep its vibrant purple color when cooked rather than turning brown. Once steamed, the eggplant becomes a blank canvas ready to absorb flavor—in this case, a Japanese mirin-and-miso sauce topped with salty crunches of fried quinoa.

EGGPLANT

4 cups water

2 tablespoons white vinegar

4 medium Chinese eggplants, trimmed

SAUCE

1/2 cup mirin

2 tablespoons white miso

1 tablespoon light brown sugar

Makes 2 servings

QUINOA

1/2 cup uncooked quinoa

1/3 cup vegetable oil

TOPPINGS

Finely chopped scallions

Kosher salt

PREP AND SOAK THE EGGPLANT: In a large mixing bowl, stir together the water and vinegar. Quarter an eggplant lengthwise, then cut each quarter in half crosswise to get 8 wedges total. Repeat for the remaining eggplants. Immediately place the eggplant slices in the bowl and soak until ready to steam, up to 10 minutes.

MAKE THE SAUCE: In a small saucepan, heat the mirin over medium heat until it boils, then reduce the heat to low. Mix in the miso and brown sugar and stir until the sauce has thickened slightly and become smooth. Set aside.

BOIL AND FRY THE QUINOA: In a small saucepan with a lid, combine the quinoa and 1 cup water and bring to a boil. Reduce the heat to maintain a gentle simmer, cover, and cook for 20 minutes, until the quinoa has sprouted and is tender and the water has evaporated. Once the quinoa is cooked, transfer to a plate to dry out for 10 minutes. In a medium skillet, warm the oil over medium-high heat, then add the quinoa and stir. Cook until it sizzles and reaches a medium golden brown, about 5 minutes. Transfer to a wide, shallow dish or a plate lined with a paper towel.

STEAM THE EGGPLANT AND ASSEMBLE THE DISH: Remove the eggplant slices from the water and transfer them to a bamboo steamer. Fill a pot that will fit your bamboo steamer with an inch of water and bring to a boil. Place the steamer in the pot and cover. Steam the eggplant for 8 minutes, until soft. In a large mixing bowl, combine the eggplant and the mirin-and-miso sauce and toss lightly. Serve with a generous sprinkling of fried quinoa, scallions, and salt to taste.

My parents were raised alongside the night markets of Taipei, where cramped stalls lit by red lanterns turned out succulent marinated chicken encased in a crisp golden-brown crust. Twenty years later, they shared their fried chicken ritual with me . . . except mine was delivered through a drive-through window in a box labeled Chicken McNuggets with a side of honey mustard. This recipe is a love letter to all the fried chickens that came before me. The chicken is prepared just like my parents remember the Taiwanese night markets doing it, using sweet potato starch (found at Asian grocery stores or Amazon) to give it its characteristic crunch. It's then tossed with salt, pepper, and a honey mustard–soy glaze for a salty and tangy finish.

MARINATE THE CHICKEN: Cut the chicken thighs into halves (for smaller pieces) or thirds (for larger pieces) so you have roughly even chunks. In a large mixing bowl, stir together the garlic, soy sauce, cooking wine, salt, flour, and egg white. Add the chicken pieces, cover the bowl, and marinate in the fridge for at least 1 hour and up to overnight.

MAKE THE GLAZE: In a small bowl, whisk together the salt, honey, soy sauce, and mustard and set aside.

COAT THE CHICKEN: Pour the sweet potato starch into a large mixing bowl. Remove the chicken from the marinade. Dip a chicken piece into the starch, turning to coat, and then set aside on a plate. Repeat for all the chicken pieces.

FRY THE CHICKEN: Fill a large Dutch oven or heavy pot with 2 to 3 cups of oil (to reach a depth of about 3 inches) and throw in a handful of basil. Set over high heat and warm until the oil temperature reaches 350° to 375°F. The oil is ready when you start to see a light simmering of bubbles around the basil leaves. Take the basil out with a mesh strainer, set aside for garnish, and turn the heat down to low-medium.

Fry the chicken in batches, turning as necessary, until lightly golden brown, 2 to 3 minutes per batch. Remove the chicken pieces with a mesh strainer and transfer to the prepared tray lined with paper towels. When all the chicken has had its first fry, turn the heat up to high to get the oil to 385 to 395°F. For the final fry, place the chicken pieces back in the pot and flash-fry for 30 seconds to 1 minute, until golden brown. Transfer the chicken back to paper towels to drain. In a large mixing bowl, toss the chicken with a sprinkle of salt and pepper.

GLAZE THE CHICKEN: Pour the glaze into the bowl with the fried chicken and toss until evenly coated. Top the chicken with sesame seeds, garnish with fried basil, and serve warm.

HONEY MUSTARD–GLAZED TAIWANESE POPCORN CHICKEN

CHICKEN

2 pounds boneless, skinless chicken thighs

3 garlic cloves, minced

1 tablespoon soy sauce

2 tablespoons Shaoxing wine, mirin, or sake

1 teaspoon kosher salt

2 tablespoons all-purpose flour

1 egg white

14 ounces sweet potato starch

2 to 3 cups canola oil, vegetable oil, or any other oil with a high smoke point

1 handful of fresh basil leaves

Freshly ground black pepper

GLAZE

3 teaspoons kosher salt

3 tablespoons honey

2 teaspoons soy sauce

3 teaspoons Dijon mustard

TOPPINGS

Black or white sesame seeds

Makes 3 servings

FAN TUAN WITH TOMATO EGG

Sitting in the back seat of my dad's minivan, I'm handed an open plastic bag. Inside sits a large cylinder of sticky rice, its warmth radiating through the plastic. I shimmy the plastic down and take a small bite. I'm greeted with a warm stickiness from the rice along with an unexpected crunch—a fried cruller also known as youtiao in all its golden-brown crispiness. My bite also reveals sweetness from pork floss, while specks of green tell me the acid cutting through the youtiao's satisfying grease is pickled mustard greens.

This Taiwanese breakfast staple of varied textures and flavors is called fan tuan. It's found in breakfast shops all over Taiwan, packaged in an unassuming plastic bag. With this recipe, I wanted to re-create traditional fan tuan using some of my favorite fillings. Stir-fried tomato egg is the main event, its savory-sweet coating of tomatoes and ginger the perfect accompaniment to sticky rice. Traditional youtiao adds heartiness and crunch, while simple pickled radishes round out the filling, providing a balance of acid.

The best part of fan tuan is that any of its fillings can be eaten individually. Stir-fried tomato egg goes great with a bowl of rice. Youtiao on its own or in a bowl of congee makes a comforting meal. Extra radishes are a great topping for savory dishes or a condiment for sandwiches. The pickles can be made a day or two in advance.

TOMATO EGGS

6 eggs

1 tablespoon chicken stock

½ teaspoon toasted sesame oil

1½ teaspoons kosher salt

4 tablespoons vegetable oil

4 scallions, green and white parts chopped

½ teaspoon grated fresh ginger

1 teaspoon grated garlic (about 3 cloves)

¾ pound tomatoes (about 2 large beefsteak), cut into 1-inch chunks

½ teaspoon granulated sugar

2 tablespoons ketchup

YOUTIAO

5 youtiao (Chinese crullers)

Canola oil, vegetable oil, or any other oil with a high smoke point

RADISH PICKLES

8 small radishes, trimmed and thinly sliced

1 tablespoon granulated sugar

1½ teaspoons kosher salt

1 recipe Sticky Rice (page 103)

Makes 3 to 4 fan tuan

MAKE THE TOMATO EGGS: In a medium mixing bowl, beat the eggs with the chicken stock, sesame oil, and ½ teaspoon of the salt. In a medium saucepan, warm 2 tablespoons of the vegetable oil over high heat. When the oil is just about to smoke, carefully add the eggs and stir continuously until they firm up, 30 to 45 seconds. Transfer the eggs to a bowl, then wipe down the pan. Warm the remaining 2 tablespoons vegetable oil in the same pan over medium-high heat. Add the scallions, ginger, and garlic and stir continuously until fragrant, about 10 seconds. Add the tomatoes and continue to cook, stirring occasionally, for 2 to 3 minutes, until the tomatoes have started to break down a bit and their juices begin to simmer. Reduce the heat to low and add the remaining 1 teaspoon salt, the sugar, and the ketchup. Mix until fully incorporated, then return the eggs to the pan and stir to fold the eggs into the sauce. Set aside until ready to assemble the fan tuan.

PAN-FRY THE YOUTIAO: In a medium saucepan or skillet over medium heat, warm a generous glug of oil. Pan-fry the youtiao so they're crispy all over, about 1 minute per side. Remove from the heat and set on some paper towels to drain and cool. Cut in half widthwise and set aside until ready to assemble the fan tuan.

MAKE THE RADISH PICKLES: In a small mixing bowl, combine the radishes, sugar, and salt, and lightly massage all the individual slices. Let the radishes sit for 10 minutes to let the salt pull the water out. Squeeze the radishes and drain the excess water from the mixing bowl, and then put the radishes in the fridge until ready to use. You can do this a day or two in advance if preferred.

continued

FAN TUAN WITH TOMATO EGG

continued

ASSEMBLE THE FAN TUAN: Now that all the ingredients are ready, it's time to assemble. Lay out a large piece of plastic wrap on a work surface. Using a plastic rice paddle or silicone spatula, scoop some sticky rice onto the plastic wrap. Use the flat end of the rice paddle and firmly press down on the rice to create a thin layer. Keep scooping small amounts of rice and thinly spreading it until it's approximately a 6 by 10-inch rectangle.

In the center of the sticky rice, add a cut youtiao, a scoop of scrambled tomato egg, and a row of pickles, leaving a couple inches around the ingredients so you have room to roll it up. Using the plastic wrap, roll up the rice to enclose the ingredients and make a burrito-like shape. Close off the two ends by squeezing the rice together. Keep tightening the rice around the ingredients, using the plastic wrap to seal everything into place. Serve the fan tuan right away, wrapped in plastic. If saving for later, seal in plastic and store in the fridge for up to 3 days. To reheat, remove the plastic wrap, wrap in a damp paper towel, and heat in the microwave for 30 to 45 seconds to soften the sticky rice.

I love that so many Asian cultures have a version of the steamed egg. Chinese zheng dan (蒸蛋), Korean gyeranjjim (계란찜), Japanese chawanmushi (茶碗蒸し): all delicious in their own ways. The perfect steamed egg is known for its smooth texture with a slight jiggle, achieved through steaming a mixture of egg and liquid at a low temperature. My grandma loves using broth for her steamed eggs, and I've found that bone broth, with its additional collagen, especially enhances the custard texture. The most challenging part of this whole recipe is the steaming. Cook too hot and the egg custard will become hard and bubbly instead of smooth and moist. Cook too low and you'll have the perfect custard but at a snail's pace. Every stove is its own special snowflake, so it will take some trial and error to find the right amount of heat to achieve peak custard texture. I recommend setting your burner right between low and medium and cooking for 14 to 16 minutes. If it takes much more or less time than that, adjust the heat for the next time you make it. The mirin in the recipe is optional but adds a slight sweetness that balances out the salt.

GRANDMA'S STEAMED EGG

MAKE THE EGG MIXTURE: Crack the egg into a small mixing bowl and whisk well with chopsticks. Add the bone broth, salt, soy sauce, and mirin (if using) and mix together until fully incorporated. Pour the egg mixture through a fine-mesh metal sieve into a heatproof soup bowl that will fit in a steamer.

STEAM THE EGG: Insert a bamboo or metal steamer on top of a shallow pan filled with water. Bring the water to a simmer over medium-high heat, then turn the heat to low-medium. Place the soup bowl with the egg mixture into your steamer above the water and cover the steamer with a lid. Steam for 14 to 16 minutes, until the egg mixture has set and the surface is smooth and jiggly. Remove the bowl, top the egg with chopped scallions and a drizzle of soy sauce, and serve.

1 egg

³⁄₄ cup chicken bone broth (store-bought or homemade)

¹⁄₄ teaspoon kosher salt

¹⁄₂ teaspoon soy sauce

¹⁄₄ teaspoon mirin (optional)

Chopped scallions for garnish

Soy sauce for garnish

Makes 1 bowl

STEAMED EGG TOPPINGS

Basil leaves, rosemary flowers, scallions, Scallion Oil (page 11), fennel fronds, togorashi

Shrimp, candied pecans, scallions, corn

Sautéed mushrooms, squash, chives, chervil

Bacon, apple, chives

BING

Coming Out

Hey Dad,

I haven't talked to you in seven years.

I'm pan-frying bing on the stove in my kitchen in Seattle (that's where I live now) just like how Grandma taught you. Cooking these fragrant flatbreads reminds me of our past life. A life I'm seemingly starting to forget as the years trail by. I remember you filling the kitchen week after week with the same smell of fried oil. Mom used to always complain about it seeping into my clothes, making me smell more "Asian" to the white kids at school.

"So what? We are Asian," you always said. I'm getting better at saying that myself.

It's funny how food forces me to confront the existences of the people in life who aren't in my life anymore. Every time I eat vanilla wafers I think of Joel. Remember my friend from grade school? I was eight years old when he showed me the magic of dipping vanilla wafers in shitty lemonade while also teaching me the word *vagina*. I got sent to the principal's office a day later after joyfully screaming "vagina!" in a five-year-old's face during silent reading time. I never told you that.

Even a bite of watermelon still reminds me of the last girl I ever went on a date with. She was an extroverted designer who stared into my eyes and wholeheartedly insisted that my soul was reincarnated from a ripe watermelon (and hers from an avocado). I started dating boys after that. I never told you that either.

I guess this is my coming-out to you. I hope this isn't too big a surprise. I remember the only requests you had for me were to never do drugs, to not become a starving artist, and to marry an intelligent woman. Clearly a lot has changed since we talked about the future together. I make bing now, in the same way you taught me, for my boyfriend, Scott. He's an intelligent man instead of a woman, but I hope you would've been proud all the same. He reads a lot just like you and has a penchant (also like you) for reminding me not to leave on every goddamn light switch in the house. I like to think you would've bonded over that.

I'm also happy to report that I'm not starving. In fact, I'm pretty much full all the time. I'm pouring my heart and soul and flour into a cookbook. It requires me to travel back in time for my job. I cook scallion pancakes to remember the sound of your voice, even though it makes me want to cry. I'll also make dishes like the shaobing with beef tendon from House of Sun to hear your laugh. Remember all those brunches we had there after church? There was that one time when the waitress proudly announced, in Mandarin, the name of the grandest dish we ordered— but pronounced the word *chicken* as if she were saying *dick*. Mom has the unique talent of making anything into a dick joke, and the waitress literally handed it to her on a bowl of "sizzling, juicy chicken dick" topped with crackling rice. As put-together as you were, you really loved Mom's dick jokes.

It's a dream come true to cook the dishes of our past life, but as someone who's inherited your ability to avoid vulnerability throughout a lifetime, I'm also terrified. I'm terrified of what people will think of me. I'm terrified of undoing years of work building this carefully constructed facade, a sheen of perfection through filters and carefully chosen snippets of my life on a screen. The truth is, my life is far from perfect. Since your death, I've found that life has been a juxtaposition of happiness and sadness all scribbled together in the same messy drawing. It's left me searching for you everywhere I go: in my goals, my hopes, my dreams, and the food I cook. Who am I now if I'm not my father's son?

I guess it's time to find out.

Love,

Frankie

SCALLION
PANCAKES

蔥油餅

I remember once when I was a teenager, my dad packed scallion pancakes in my cooler for a camping trip with friends. He knew it was my favorite thing he cooked, a weekly treat so flaky with layers of dough and scallions that I'd eat two whole ones before dinner even started. He kneaded and pan-fried them the night before, neatly packing them into a zip-top bag for me to heat over a campfire. I got to the campsite and threw them straight in the trash, wiping their existence from the cooler before any of my friends could see.

The overwhelming joy I feel with every chewy bite of this dish has a story: The story of my dad learning this same recipe from his mom, chopping scallions alongside her in a cramped kitchen in Taipei. The story of small metal carts on Yongkang Street with Taiwanese grandmas kneading and pan-frying dough with the energy of boxers. A story of being Taiwanese that I wasn't ready to tell because it meant I had to acknowledge joy in my own heritage.

I've worked hard to replace shame with pride over the course of my adulthood. Pride in the tradition of forming the dough into its signature layers. Pride in the aroma of scallion and oil that seeps into my clothing as the scallions hit the sizzling pan. A dish that is synonymous with the comfort of being so full I can barely eat dinner. Whether eaten on its own or topped with fillings like a soft egg omelet (page 71) or marinated pork (page 78), this distinctly Taiwanese dish is worthy of being shared with everyone. See page 59 for step-by-step illustrations for making these pancakes.

DOUGH

2 cups all-purpose flour

Kosher salt

1/2 cup plus 2 tablespoons boiling water

3 tablespoons water, at room temperature

1 teaspoon canola oil or grapeseed oil, plus more for oiling and frying

Makes 3 pancakes

FLOUR AND SCALLION OIL SPREAD

4 scallions, green and white parts, chopped

1 teaspoon kosher salt

1 1/2 tablespoons all-purpose flour

1/2 cup canola oil or grapeseed oil (or any neutral oil)

MIX THE DOUGH: In a large mixing bowl, mix together the flour and 3/4 teaspoon salt. Slowly pour the boiling water into the flour mixture, stirring with a silicone spatula as you pour. Mix until it forms small chunks of dough, then add the room-temperature water and mix until incorporated.

KNEAD AND DO THE FIRST REST: Transfer the dough to a lightly floured work surface and knead for 10 minutes, or until the dough is one smooth ball. You should be able to press your finger into it and it should have some tackiness and slightly bounce back. Cover the dough in plastic wrap and let rest for 20 minutes at room temperature.

DIVIDE AND DO A SECOND REST: Uncover the dough and pour the oil on it. Knead until the oil is fully incorporated and the dough is smooth once more. Roll the dough into a log and then cut it crosswise into 3 pieces. Use your palm to flatten each piece of dough into a rough circle. Lightly oil each dough circle, then cover the dough with plastic wrap and let it rest for 1 hour at room temperature.

MAKE THE FLOUR AND SCALLION OIL SPREAD: While the dough is resting, place the scallions, salt, and flour in a heatproof bowl. In a small saucepan, warm the oil over medium heat until it starts to sizzle. Remove from the heat and very carefully pour the hot oil into the heatproof bowl to flash-fry the scallions and bring out their flavor. Stir the scallion oil and set aside.

continued

SCALLION PANCAKES

continued

FORM THE PANCAKES: When the dough has finished resting, uncover the dough circles and use a rolling pin to roll each into a flat, thin oval. Spoon an even coating of scallion oil onto each dough oval, then lightly sprinkle the surface with salt. Roll the dough tightly, starting from the long side, so it becomes a long snake. Starting from one end of the snake, coil the dough like a cinnamon roll. When you reach the end of the roll, tuck the end of the dough under the bottom of the roll to seal.

With your palm, press down firmly onto your coiled dough to flatten (or use a rolling pin). Flatten until the dough has reached your desired size (6 to 8 inches in diameter for a thinner pancake, 4 to 5 inches for a thicker one). Repeat with the remaining pieces of dough. (Tip: stack the pancakes with layers of parchment paper in between so they don't stick together.)

COOK THE PANCAKES: In a medium nonstick pan, warm a glug of oil over medium heat. Place 1 pancake into the pan and cook until lightly browned on each side, 6 to 8 minutes total. Repeat for the remaining pancakes. Cut into wedges and serve. If you don't want to cook all the scallion pancakes, layer parchment paper between each raw, rolled-out scallion pancake. Place the stack into a plastic freezer bag and freeze for up to 2 months. To cook, just pan-fry directly from frozen in an oiled pan until browned.

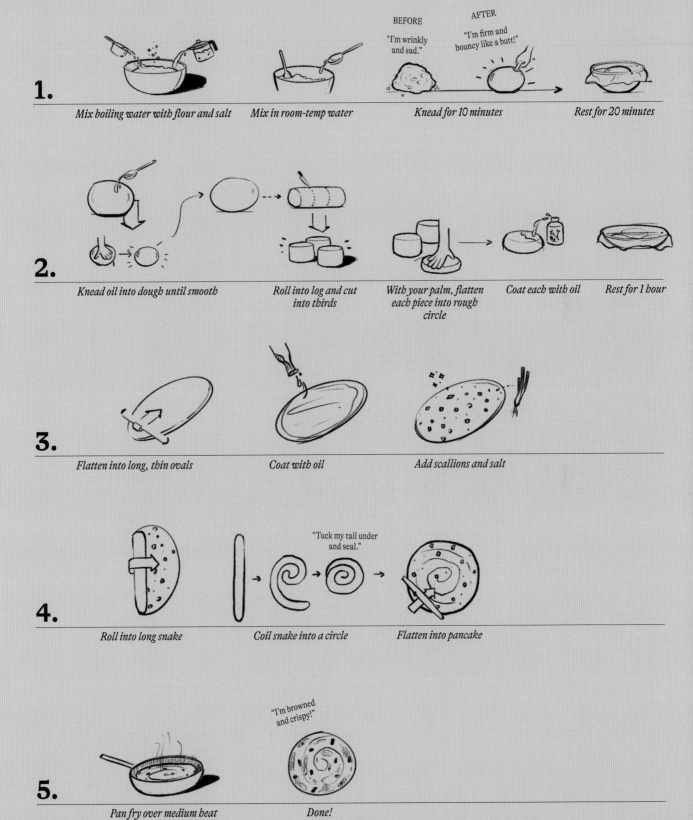

1.

Mix boiling water with flour and salt

Mix in room-temp water

BEFORE
"I'm wrinkly and sad."

AFTER
"I'm firm and bouncy like a butt!"

Knead for 10 minutes

Rest for 20 minutes

2.

Knead oil into dough until smooth

Roll into log and cut into thirds

With your palm, flatten each piece into rough circle

Coat each with oil

Rest for 1 hour

3.

Flatten into long, thin ovals

Coat with oil

Add scallions and salt

4.

Roll into long snake

Coil snake into a circle

"Tuck my tail under and seal."

Flatten into pancake

5.

Pan fry over medium heat

"I'm browned and crispy!"

Done!

Big bing is a leavened version of the scallion pancake, and one of my grandma's favorite recipes to cook for me whenever I visited her in Memphis. It's one of those dishes that tends to stay within the confines of many Taiwanese American families' homes; it's not nearly as known in America as the scallion pancake. Big bing shares a lot of the same distinct characteristics of the scallion pancake—the same kneading-and-rolling process, the use of scallions and oil to create layers within the dough. Where it differs is in technique and texture. Yeast allows the dough to come alive, creating a loaf of layered bread much larger than the typical scallion pancake. It's cooked in a covered shallow pan, where it rises, allowing it to both pan-fry and steam to impart its signature crispy outer shell and moist, doughy interior. See pages 62–63 for step-by-step photos for making Big Bing.

PREP DOUGH AND DO FIRST PROOF: In a small mixing bowl, combine the yeast and sugar. Mix in the warm water to activate the yeast, and let the mixture sit for 5 minutes, until it foams. In a large mixing bowl, combine the flour, ½ teaspoon salt, and yeast mixture and mix until it forms a rough ball. Transfer the dough to a lightly floured work surface and knead until smooth, about 10 minutes. Place the dough back into the mixing bowl and cover with plastic wrap. Proof in a warm, draft-free place for 30 minutes, until it has doubled in size.

MAKE THE FLOUR AND SCALLION OIL SPREAD: While the dough is proofing, place the scallions, salt, and flour in a heatproof bowl. In a small saucepan, warm the oil over medium heat until it starts to sizzle. Remove from the heat and very carefully pour the hot oil into the heatproof bowl to flash-fry the scallions and bring out their flavor. Stir the scallion oil and set aside.

FORM THE PANCAKE: When the dough is ready, uncover and transfer to a lightly floured work surface, and use a rolling pin to roll into a large, flat oval. Spread the scallion oil onto the dough in an even layer, then lightly sprinkle the surface with salt. Roll the dough tightly, starting from the long side, so it becomes a long snake. Starting from one end of the snake, coil the dough like a cinnamon roll. When you reach the end of the roll, tuck the end of the dough under the bottom of the roll to seal. Cover and proof for 1 hour.

COOK THE PANCAKE: Uncover the dough, brush the top with a light layer of oil, then sprinkle with a generous amount of sesame seeds. In a medium nonstick pan with a lid, warm the oil over low-medium heat. Cook the pancake, uncovered, for 6 to 10 minutes, until the bottom has lightly browned. Flip the pancake, then add 2 tablespoons water around the sides to create steam. Cover the pan and cook the pancake for another 10 minutes, until the bottom has lightly browned. Remove the pancake from the pan and cut into wedges. Serve immediately.

BIG BING

大餅

DOUGH

2 teaspoons active dry yeast

¼ teaspoon granulated sugar

1 cup warm water (95° to 110°F)

2½ cups bread flour

Kosher salt

Canola oil or grapeseed oil, for oiling and frying

FLOUR AND SCALLION OIL SPREAD

4 scallions, green and white parts, chopped

1 teaspoon kosher salt

1½ tablespoons bread or all-purpose flour

½ cup canola oil or grapeseed oil (or any neutral oil)

TOPPING

Sesame seeds

Makes 1 large pancake

DAN BING

蛋餅

(Taiwanese Egg Crepes)

Dan bing is a traditional Taiwanese breakfast dish that my grandma used to make for me in the mornings. It's a thin pancake almost like a crepe, full of egg flavor and springy in texture, with crisp, oily edges that I fondly savor. This dish always transported me to Taipei, even though I couldn't remember what it was like there. I loved hearing about Taipei's breakfast shops, their dan bing and soy milk feeding bustling lines of workers looking for a comforting breakfast to start the day. Dan bing is the simplest dish in this entire book, requiring just a quick whisk of flour, water, and egg before it's cooked on a skillet. It's delicious on its own, but for a heartier dish, you can use the bing as a wrapper for any combination of your favorite ingredients, from deli meats and lettuce to stewed meats and pickles.

BATTER	SAUCE
½ cup all-purpose flour	2 tablespoons soy sauce
½ cup water	1 tablespoon honey
4 eggs	2 teaspoons water
Grapeseed oil or olive oil	Chopped scallions for garnish
Kosher salt	Sesame seeds for garnish

Makes 4 pancakes

MAKE THE BATTER: In a medium mixing bowl, whisk together the flour and water until smooth. Add the eggs and continue to whisk until everything is incorporated.

In a medium nonstick skillet, warm 1 tablespoon oil over medium heat. Once the pan is hot, pour just enough batter to thinly coat the entire surface of the pan, moving the pan around to spread evenly. As the batter firms up on the bottom, flip the pancake to cook the other side. Continue to flip until very lightly browned and cooked through. Sprinkle with a little salt, then set aside on a plate. Repeat with the remaining batter until all four pancakes are cooked.

MAKE THE SAUCE: In a small mixing bowl, whisk together the soy sauce, honey, and water until smooth.

To serve, roll the pancakes into tubes and cut into 4 to 5 slices. Drizzle with the sweet soy sauce, top with chopped scallions and sesame seeds, and serve.

This unleavened, baked flatbread filled with thin layers of dough and topped with sesame seeds is perfectly handheld and characteristically flaky, its voyage to one's mouth always leaving a trail of crisp crumbs. I first encountered this bing at House of Sun, a small Chinese restaurant my parents would take us to every Sunday after church. An order of shaobing on the table was always a sign that Taiwanese brunch season was upon us. Its clamshell opening makes it the perfect vehicle for fillings like simple scrambled egg for breakfast, marinated short rib with pickles and cilantro (page 77) for brunch, or really any type of filling that suits your fancy. See page 69 for step-by-step illustrations for making these pancakes.

SESAME SHAOBING

芝麻燒餅
(Baked Layered Sesame Flatbread)

DOUGH	FLOUR AND OIL PASTE
2½ cups bread flour	½ cup olive oil
Kosher salt	2 tablespoons bread flour
¾ cup boiling water	
¼ cup water, at room temperature	
1 egg	
Sesame seeds for topping	

Makes 8 shaobing

MIX THE DOUGH AND REST: In a large mixing bowl, stir together the flour and 1 teaspoon salt. Slowly pour in the boiling water, stirring with a silicone spatula as you pour. Add the room-temperature water and continue to mix until clumps form. Transfer to a lightly floured work surface and knead until the dough forms a rough ball. Cover in plastic wrap and let rest for 15 to 20 minutes. Uncover and knead again until the dough is completely smooth, about 5 minutes. Cover again with plastic wrap and let rest for another 30 minutes to allow the dough to fully relax.

MAKE THE FLOUR AND OIL PASTE: While the dough is resting, in a small mixing bowl, mix the oil and flour with a fork. Set aside.

SHAPE THE SHAOBING: After the dough has rested, use a rolling pin to flatten it on a work surface into a large square, approximately 15 by 15 inches.

SPREAD THE FLOUR AND OIL PASTE: Using the back of a spoon or a silicone brush, spread an even layer of the flour-and-oil paste across the surface of the dough. Season with a light sprinkling of salt.

ROLL THE DOUGH INTO A SNAKE: Starting from one end, tightly roll the dough like a cinnamon roll into a long snake.

CUT THE DOUGH: Cut the dough into 8 equal pieces.

FLATTEN THE DOUGH: Place a dough piece with the seam side down on a working surface while the cut sides are facing up and down. Use a rolling pin to roll the dough into a 3 by 6-inch rectangle. Repeat for all pieces of dough.

FOLD THE DOUGH: Fold a rectangle widthwise into thirds by folding each edge inward toward the center. Use a rolling pin to roll into a square. Repeat for all pieces of dough.

FLATTEN AGAIN: Fold a square in half with the seams on the inside and lightly flatten to shape into a 3 by 6-inch rectangle. Repeat for all pieces of dough.

continued

SESAME SHAOBING

continued

ADD EGG WASH AND SESAME SEEDS: Line two baking sheets with parchment paper. In a small mixing bowl, scramble the egg. Pour a thin layer of sesame seeds onto a plate. Use a pastry brush or silicone brush to evenly brush the top of the dough with the beaten egg. Invert the bing into the plate of sesame seeds so the seeds adhere to the egg wash, then set the dough on the baking sheet, seeds facing up. Repeat for all pieces of dough.

BAKE THE SHAOBING: Preheat the oven to 425°F. Bake the shaobing for 20 minutes, until lightly risen and browned. Serve as is, or split in half to add toppings of your choice. Store in a sealed freezer bag for up to 3 months. To reheat, just toast in the oven at 375°F for 10 minutes or wrap in a damp paper towel and heat for 1 minute in the microwave.

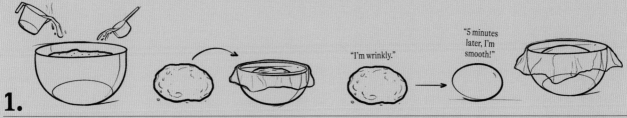

1. Mix boiling water then room temp water | Knead into a rough ball then cover and rest for 15 to 20 minutes | Uncover and knead until smooth | Cover and rest for another 30 minutes

"I'm wrinkly."

"5 minutes later, I'm smooth!"

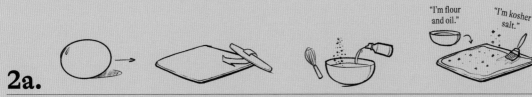

2a. Roll into flat square-ish shape | Mix flour and oil together | Spread evenly

"I'm flour and oil."

"I'm kosher salt."

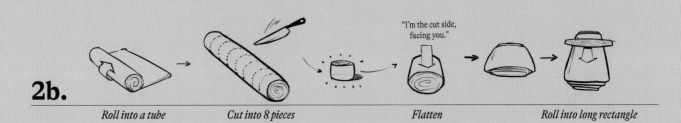

2b. Roll into a tube | Cut into 8 pieces | Flatten | Roll into long rectangle

"I'm the cut side, facing you."

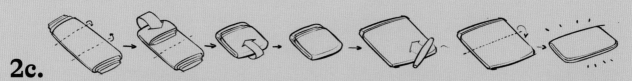

2c. Fold into thirds | Flatten into 6-inch square | Then fold in half

3. Brush egg wash on top | Sprinkle sesame seeds | Bake

Scallion pancakes were destined to be paired with an egg; the pancake's flat layered dough is the perfect landing spot for a filling. This recipe is Taiwanese homestyle breakfast at its most comforting, a common preparation made by many an auntie or grandma. Beaten egg is poured in a hot oiled pan, and just before the egg sets, a scallion pancake is placed on top, binding the two together for a perfect bite of soft egg, crisp scallion pancake, and savory comfort.

In a small mixing bowl, beat the eggs and set aside. In a small nonstick pan, warm a glug of oil over medium heat. Place the pancake into the pan and cook on both sides to warm, then transfer to a plate. While the pan is still hot, add 1 tablespoon oil and sprinkle the scallions into the pan to flash fry, about 30 seconds. Pour the beaten egg over the scallions and lightly stir them with a chopstick to even out the egg and spread it around the pan as it continues to cook. When the eggs have reached a half liquid, half solid form (about 30 seconds), add the warmed scallion pancake on top and continue cooking until the egg has cooked through, another minute or so. Flip the pancake and egg together so the egg mixture is face-up, and top with a light sprinkle of salt. Remove from the pan and tightly roll from one end to the other. Cut the rolled pancake into diagonal strips and serve.

SCALLION PANCAKE WITH EGG OMELET

2 eggs

Canola oil or
vegetable oil

1 Scallion Pancake
(page 56)

2 scallions, green
and white parts,
chopped

Kosher salt

Makes 1 serving

RED PEPPER SCALLION PANCAKES WITH RED PEPPER PASTE

This recipe was inspired by going over to friends' homes as a child, and all the sports on TV there that I couldn't care less about. The repetitive back-and-forth of men in tights throwing a brown thing on a screen was a mere backdrop to the main event I'd shown up for: the delicious spread of finger food, ready for the taking. Specifically, my heart had a special bond with nachos and dips, dishes that were a rare sight in my household. Those snacks led me to this scallion pancake, in which red bell peppers make a nontraditional guest appearance. Each bite delivers those familiar flaky layers distinct in scallion pancakes, with a hint of acid from the peppers. A cashew crema and red bell pepper dip round out this tribute to the nachos of my childhood; it's great on the side or drizzled all over the scallion pancakes. See pages 74–75 for step-by-step photos for making these pancakes.

BELL PEPPER DIP

3 red bell peppers, stemmed, seeded, and coarsely chopped

¼ cup olive oil

1 teaspoon kosher salt

1 teaspoon maple syrup

1 teaspoon balsamic vinegar

2 tablespoons water

½ teaspoon red pepper flakes

DOUGH

2 cups all-purpose flour

¾ teaspoon kosher salt

¾ cup plus 1 tablespoon red bell pepper water, from blending the bell peppers

1 teaspoon canola oil, plus more for oiling and frying

Makes 3 pancakes

FLOUR AND SCALLION OIL SPREAD

4 scallions, green and white parts, chopped

1 teaspoon kosher salt

1½ tablespoons all-purpose flour

½ cup canola oil or grapeseed oil (or any neutral oil)

TOPPINGS

Scallion Cashew Cream (page 12)

Chopped scallions

White or black sesame seeds

MAKE THE BELL PEPPER DIP: In a blender, blend the peppers until smooth. (Red bell peppers hold quite a bit of water, but if they aren't blending smoothly, add water, 1 tablespoon at a time.) Strain the mixture through a fine-mesh metal sieve, reserving solids and liquids separately. Set the strained liquid (red bell pepper water) aside to use in the dough. In a small saucepan, combine the bell pepper solids and the olive oil. Cook over medium heat, stirring occasionally, for 5 minutes, until the mixture simmers and thickens. Add the salt, maple syrup, balsamic vinegar, water, and red pepper flakes and cook, stirring, until the mixture is a thick, vibrant orange paste, 3 to 5 minutes. Transfer to a heatproof container, cover, and store in the fridge until ready to use. You can make this up to 2 days in advance.

MIX THE DOUGH: Mix together the flour and salt in a large mixing bowl. In a small saucepan, bring ½ cup plus 2 tablespoons of the red bell pepper water to a boil. Remove from the heat and slowly pour the liquid into the flour mixture, stirring as you pour. Mix until it forms small chunks of dough. Add the remaining 3 tablespoons red bell pepper water and mix into the dough until incorporated.

KNEAD AND DO THE FIRST REST: Transfer the dough to a lightly floured work surface and knead for 10 minutes, or until the dough is one smooth vibrant-orange ball. You should be able to press your finger into it and it should have some tackiness and slightly bounce back. Cover the dough in plastic wrap and let rest for 20 minutes at room temperature.

DIVIDE AND DO A SECOND REST: Uncover the dough and pour 1 teaspoon canola oil on it. Knead until the oil is fully incorporated and the dough is smooth once more. Roll the dough into a log, and then cut it crosswise into 3 pieces. Use your palm to flatten each piece of dough into a rough circle. Lightly oil each dough circle, then cover with plastic wrap and let rest for 1 hour at room temperature.

MAKE THE FLOUR AND SCALLION OIL SPREAD: While the dough is resting, place the scallions, salt, and flour in a heatproof bowl. In a small saucepan, warm the oil over medium heat until it starts to sizzle. Remove from the heat and very carefully pour the hot oil into the heatproof bowl to flash-fry the scallions and bring out their flavor. Stir the scallion oil and set aside.

continued

RED PEPPER SCALLION PANCAKES WITH RED PEPPER PASTE

continued

FORM THE PANCAKES: When the dough has finished resting, uncover the dough circles and use a rolling pin to roll each into a flat, thin oval. Spoon an even coating of scallion oil onto each dough oval, then lightly sprinkle with salt. Roll the dough tightly, starting from the long side, so it becomes a long snake. Starting from one end of the snake, coil the dough like a cinnamon roll. When you reach the end of the roll, tuck the end of the dough under the bottom of the roll to seal.

With your palm, press down firmly onto your coiled dough to flatten (or use a rolling pin). Flatten until the dough has reached your desired size (6 to 8 inches in diameter for a thinner pancake, 4 to 5 inches for a thicker one). Repeat with the remaining pieces of dough. (Tip: stack the pancakes with layers of parchment paper in between so they don't stick together.)

COOK THE PANCAKES: In a medium nonstick pan, warm a glug of oil over medium heat. Place 1 pancake in the pan and cook on both sides until each side is lightly browned, 6 to 8 minutes total. Repeat for the remaining pancakes. Cut into wedges and serve with a generous drizzle of cashew cream and red bell pepper dip spread throughout. Sprinkle with the chopped scallions and sesame seeds, and serve.

In this recipe, shaobing meets its old friends, marinated beef shank and fresh cilantro; this classic combination is found in sandwich form in many Taiwanese restaurants and family gatherings alike. For me, it's a dish that brings back memories of its place on the table alongside Taiwanese brunch classics like savory soy milk and the fried crullers known as youtiao. Shaobing with beef traditionally uses beef shank, but for this recipe I'm swapping in slow-cooked bone-in beef short ribs. It's a decadence that I could imagine Ina Garten suggesting, if she could have spoken through the TV as my grandma and I watched her cook short ribs on the Food Network. Here, the short ribs are cooked slowly in a bath of soy sauce, star anise, ginger, and orange (among other aromatics), giving the beef a classic Taiwanese flavor while imparting fall-off-the-bone tenderness.

SHAOBING WITH SLOW-COOKED SHORT RIB

BROWN THE SHORT RIBS: In a Dutch oven or an oven-safe large, heavy pot with a lid, warm a glug of oil over medium-high heat. Brown the short ribs on all sides in two batches, roughly 2 minutes per side. Transfer to a plate and set aside.

BRAISE THE VEGETABLES AND SHORT RIBS: Preheat the oven to 275°F. In the same Dutch oven, sauté the garlic, scallions, onions, and carrots for 5 to 10 minutes, until the onions have softened and are translucent. Add the salt and stir to incorporate. Add the Shaoxing wine and simmer for another few minutes to burn off the alcohol. Add the soy sauce, chicken stock, sugar, orange zest, ginger, and cinnamon and mix to combine. Finally, add the short ribs back into the pot. Bring the entire mixture to a light simmer, then cover and place in the oven for 4 hours, until the meat is fall-off-the-bone tender.

ASSEMBLE THE SHAOBING: Remove the short ribs from the pot. (Reserve the contents of the pot; see Tip below.) When the ribs are cool enough to handle, pull the meat off the bone and shred. Heat the shaobing by toasting in the oven at 375°F for 5 minutes (10 minutes if from frozen), and open in half lengthwise. Divide the meat among the shaobing and top with pickles and a heaping pile of cilantro. Serve warm.

Tip:
After removing the short ribs from the Dutch oven, strain the short rib broth, discarding the solids, and store in the fridge overnight. The next day, remove the top layer of fat, then use the broth to sauce future short ribs or to add a hearty beef flavor bomb to sautéed vegetables.

MEAT

Canola oil or vegetable oil

4 pounds English-cut short ribs

3 garlic cloves, smashed

2 scallions, green and white parts, chopped

2 yellow onions, coarsely chopped

2 medium carrots, coarsely chopped

1 teaspoon kosher salt

2 cups Shaoxing wine

¼ cup soy sauce

2 cups chicken stock

1 tablespoon granulated sugar

2 two-inch-long strips orange zest

4 thumb-sized slices ginger

1 cinnamon stick

WRAPPER

1 recipe Sesame Shaobing (page 67)

TOPPINGS

Cold Marinated Pickles (page 22)

Chopped cilantro

Makes 8 servings

SCALLION PANCAKES WITH ANCHO HOISIN PORK SHOULDER

My love of Mexican food started from the only "Mexican" restaurant I had ever seen in my suburb of Anderson Township—a restaurant by the name of Chipotle. My dad and I went weekly on Wednesdays for six years, and its carnitas burrito bowls with an extra side of tortillas fueled my way through high school. I've always felt there was a kinship between tortillas and scallion pancakes, both delicious carbs in a form made for wrapping ingredients. In this recipe, scallion pancakes serve as the base for tender slow-cooked pork shoulder marinated in a dry rub of ancho chiles, coffee, and paprika. It's topped with a nutty almond-soy glaze that emphasizes the smokiness in the pork, then is layered with rice vinegar red onions for acidity. This dish pays tribute to the suburban Chipotles of my childhood and the taquerias in San Francisco's Mission District that I discovered later in life.

DRY RUB

2 tablespoons finely ground coffee

2 tablespoons ancho chile powder

2 tablespoons dark brown sugar

1 tablespoon smoked paprika

2 teaspoons ground cumin

1/2 teaspoon cinnamon

1 tablespoon kosher salt

2 teaspoons freshly ground black pepper

2 tablespoons unsweetened cocoa

MEAT/VEGGIES

4 pounds pork butt or shoulder, cut into 4 to 6 chunks

1 sweet onion, halved

Makes 3 servings

WET MARINADE

1/4 cup maple syrup

2 tablespoons balsamic vinegar

Juice of 1 lime

1 cup chicken stock

2 tablespoons minced chipotles in adobo

WRAPPER

1 recipe Scallion Pancakes (page 56), rewarmed if necessary

TOPPINGS

Almond Soy Glaze (page 11)

Pickled onions

Chopped cilantro

PREP THE PORK: In a large mixing bowl, combine the coffee, chile powder, brown sugar, paprika, cumin, cinnamon, salt, pepper, and chocolate, and stir to mix. Place the pork in the bowl and pat it with the dry ingredients, turning it until each piece is completely covered.

MAKE THE MARINADE AND COOK THE PORK: In a medium mixing bowl, combine the maple syrup, balsamic vinegar, lime juice, chicken stock, and chipotles, and stir to combine.

Preheat the oven to 275°F. In a large Dutch oven, combine the seasoned pork and the onion halves. Pour the marinade over the pork and onions and stir to coat. Cover and cook for 4 hours, until the pork is completely tender. Transfer the pork to a plate, and shred using two forks.

MAKE THE PICKLED ONIONS: While the pork is cooking, make 1/2 recipe of Cold Marinated Pickles (page 22) using 1 medium red onion, thinly sliced, instead of cucumbers.

ASSEMBLE THE PANCAKES: On each pancake, spread a small dab of the almond soy glaze, then top with shredded pork, pickled onions, and cilantro. Serve immediately. Any extra pork can be stored in a sealed container in the fridge for up to 3 days or in the freezer for up to 6 months.

NOODLE

S AND RICE

A Pensieve of Rice and Noodles

In *Harry Potter and the Goblet of Fire* (allow me to nerd out for a second), Professor Dumbledore takes Harry to his office to view a Pensieve—a cauldron of mysterious liquid that, when you dip your head in, transports you to another dimension, a vivid memory of sorts in full view. Harry sees the characters of this memory and feels their every emotion, his mind in the present yet physically playing out the events of the past. This magic is familiar. It's a magic I notice when eating something so nostalgic it transcends the memory and its setting and dips me into a well of emotion. It explains how, when opening a rice cooker, I savor every plume of steam wafting into my face like an expensive facial. It reminds me of family. It transports me to watching my dad pour a tin of Planters Honey Roasted Peanuts on a bed of steamed white rice. I can't tell whether this dish's deliciousness stems purely from nostalgia or from actual gastronomical merit. Either way, I relish its pairing of sweet crunchiness and fluffy warm grains.

The slurp of a noodle pulls me home, to sitting at my family's kitchen table in the suburb of Anderson Township. I see my mom facing away from our worn Panasonic TV, rolling her eyes at the lack of conversation as she loudly eats her noodles covered in Prego meat sauce. My dad and I stare blindly past her grievances to enjoy the other member of our household, *Wheel of Fortune's* Pat Sajak. My dad's in deep focus as Pat announces the next category. His chopsticks flake the crisp outer edges of his tender soy-marinated salmon, intertwining it with strands of spaghetti coated in Prego for a Taiwanese/Italian/American bite that should be in a category all its own.

When I was growing up, our culinary scene existed on Beechmont Avenue, a five-mile strip of plazas frozen in the 1990s, with restaurants ranging from our beloved McDonald's to Applebee's. No restaurant on this stretch of road had more impact on our family's table than the Chez Panisse of Anderson Township—Olive Garden. It was the fanciest restaurant on Beechmont, a destination whose parking lot overflowed with Honda Odysseys. As we'd wait in anticipation to be seated, plastic pagers in hand, I'd look around and see large white families squeezed onto the wooden benches around us, four generations deep. I would dream of the impending joy of oozy white macaroni shells and cheese from the kids' menu and endless buttery breadsticks—my American Dream.

Our kitchen table began to evolve. My mom would make spaghetti, except there were way more raw carrots ("good for your eyes so you don't go blind") and way too much steamed broccoli on top ("nutrition for solid poops and growth spurts"). Olive Garden became a template our family could follow, a North Star we could use as a guide to navigate to the pinnacle of the American experience we saw in the white families surrounding us. "Fake it till you make it," my mom always used to say.

Except we were never going to be a white family. Instead, we were a mom and a dad with an only child. Immigrants with only our native tongue and just enough money to eat dinners at Burger King in the early years. A family working exponentially harder and longer than our white counterparts to be noticed, to survive, to thrive. A family navigating our identities through the dishes we ate, emulating white restaurants and white families. In doing so, we created a delicious point of view that stood all on its own. Our dishes intermingled family staples of fried rice and soy sauce with fatty deli ham from the local Kroger supermarket. Recipes paired the tradition of hand-cutting noodles, vibrant green with spinach, and slathering them with a hearty meat sauce, blurring the lines between the nonnas of Bologna and the aunties of Taipei. We were always going to be a family of our own unique identity, no matter how hard we tried not to be.

Thirteen years later, I'm in San Francisco, in a Victorian apartment in the heart of the Mission that I pay too much rent for. I'm trying to find my way back home, setting the table with dishes as if I were concocting my own magic cauldrons of memory. I set a rice cooker filled with white rice for three, even though I'm the only one home tonight. I'll stir-fry tomatoes folded between delicate scrambled eggs, despite tomatoes being out of season. Meat sauce from Lucca across the street is on the stove, warming the kitchen with an air of familiarity. Because as I build my own life now, a son without his father, I fondly cook these dishes. They're the most powerful Pensieves I have. I set the food on the table with *Wheel of Fortune* in the background, ready to be teleported like a Portkey to countless suburban nights with my mom and dad, magically whole again, even just for a moment.

FLOUR NOODLES

2 cups "00" flour
or all-purpose
flour, plus more
for dusting

3/4 cup warm water

Makes 1 pound

A simple noodle made with just flour and water. These noodles can be rolled out by hand and knife cut or made with a pasta machine.

MIX AND KNEAD THE DOUGH: Place the flour in a medium mixing bowl. Slowly pour in the water, mixing with a silicone spatula until the water is fully incorporated with the flour. Mix until rough clumps form, then remove the dough from the bowl and transfer it to a lightly floured work surface. Knead until the dough becomes smooth and the surface is uniform like a baby's butt, about 10 minutes. Wrap the dough in plastic wrap and let it rest at room temperature for 1 hour to allow the gluten to relax.

ROLL THE DOUGH WITH A PASTA MACHINE: Set your pasta machine to its thickest setting. Lightly dust a work surface with flour. When the dough is ready, unwrap it and cut it in half. With your fingers, shape each half into a rough 3 by 5-inch rectangle (it doesn't have to be exact). Feed one half of the dough through the pasta machine. Fold the dough into thirds lengthwise, taking each edge and bringing it toward the center in a letter fold. Use your fingers to shape it again into a rough 3 by 5-inch rectangle, and run it through the pasta machine again. Repeat with the other dough half.

Decrease the thickness on the pasta machine by one setting, then run one of your dough halves through. Continue to decrease the setting by one and run your dough through until you're at the fifth setting of your pasta machine or at whatever setting you like depending on how thick or thin you like your noodles.

When the dough is at the desired thickness, sprinkle with flour on both sides. Feed the dough through the cut side of the pasta machine with the desired width. Repeat with the other dough half until all the noodles have been cut. Loosely separate the noodles into strands, then dust with flour and lightly toss the noodles to coat them evenly. Cook immediately, or store in an airtight container in the fridge for up to 2 days or in the freezer for up to 6 months.

ROLL THE DOUGH WITH A ROLLING PIN: Lightly dust a work surface with flour. When the dough is ready, unwrap it and cut it in half. With a rolling pin, roll out each half until it's the size of your hand. Fold the dough into thirds lengthwise, taking each edge and bringing it toward the center in a letter fold. Use your fingers to shape it again into a rough 3 by 5-inch rectangle. Using a little elbow grease, roll out each dough half into a long rectangle that's thin enough to see the shadow or outline of your hand behind the dough.

Generously dust the rectangles of dough with flour and fold evenly lengthwise into thirds or quarters. Take a knife and evenly cut across your folded dough to the desired width to create noodles. Loosely separate the noodles into strands, then dust with flour and lightly toss the noodles to coat them evenly. Cook immediately, or store in an airtight container in the fridge for up to 2 days or in the freezer for up to 6 months.

NOODLES AND RICE

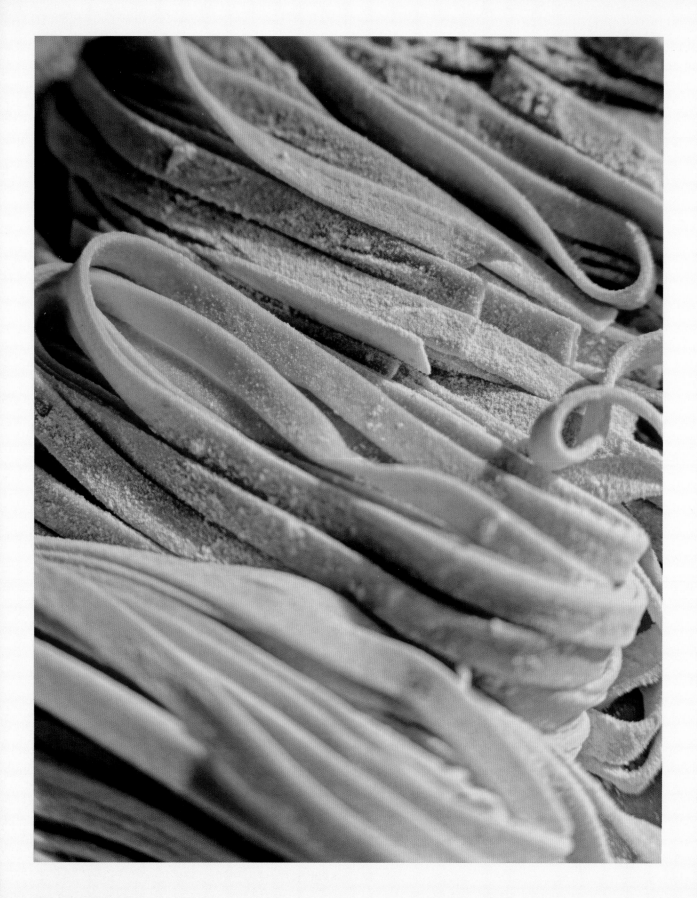

These basic egg noodles have a springy texture and work great in soups, stir-fries, or as a base for sauces. They can be made with a pasta machine or rolled out and hand-cut with a knife.

EGG NOODLES

2 cups "00" flour or all-purpose flour, plus more for dusting	Kosher salt
	3 eggs
	4 egg yolks

Makes 1 pound

MAKE THE DOUGH: Pour the flour onto a work surface and, with a fork, create a medium-sized well in the middle. Add a sprinkle of salt, crack the eggs into the well, add the yolks, and beat the eggs with the fork. As you're mixing the egg, slowly incorporate flour from the outer edges of the well until the egg and flour mix into a thick paste. Use your hands to incorporate the rest of the flour, and begin kneading the dough until it becomes smooth and the surface is uniform, like a baby's butt, about 10 minutes. Wrap the dough in plastic wrap and let it rest at room temperature for 30 minutes to 1 hour.

ROLL THE DOUGH WITH A PASTA MACHINE: Set your pasta machine to its thickest setting. Lightly dust a work surface with flour. When the dough is ready, unwrap it and cut it in half. With your fingers, shape each half into a rough 3 by 5-inch rectangle (it doesn't have to be exact). Feed one half of the dough through the pasta machine. Fold the dough into thirds lengthwise, taking each edge and bringing it toward the center in a letter fold. Use your fingers to shape it again into a rough 3 by 5-inch rectangle, and run it through the pasta machine again. Repeat with the other dough half.

Decrease the thickness on the pasta machine by one setting, then run one of your dough halves through. Continue to decrease the setting by one and run your dough through until you're at the fifth setting of the pasta machine or at whatever setting you like depending on how thick or thin you like your noodles.

When the dough is at the desired thickness, sprinkle with flour on both sides. Feed the dough through the cut side of the pasta machine with the desired width. Repeat with the other dough half until all the noodles have been cut. Loosely separate the noodles into strands, then dust with flour and lightly toss the noodles to coat them evenly. Cook immediately, or store in an airtight container in the fridge for up to 2 days or in the freezer for up to 6 months.

ROLL THE DOUGH WITH A ROLLING PIN: Lightly dust a work surface with flour. When the dough is ready, unwrap it and cut it in half. With a rolling pin, roll out each half until it's the size of your hand. Fold the dough into thirds lengthwise, taking each edge and bringing it toward the center in a letter fold. Use your fingers to shape it again into a rough 3 by 5-inch rectangle. Using a little elbow grease, roll out each dough half into a long rectangle that's thin enough to see the shadow or outline of your hand behind the dough.

Generously dust the rectangles of dough with flour and fold evenly lengthwise into thirds or quarters. Take a knife and evenly cut across your folded dough to the desired width to create noodles. Loosely separate the noodles into strands, then dust with flour and lightly toss the noodles to coat them evenly. Cook immediately, or store in an airtight container in the fridge for up to 2 days or in the freezer for up to 6 months.

HAND-PULLED NOODLES

A ritual of noodle making that requires no rolling pin or pasta machine. Hand-pulled noodles are made with just flour and water, where the dough is given time to relax before the dough is pulled in long strands of wide noodles. The practice of pulling noodles will take some time, but just know that imperfect noodles are totally okay. I personally prefer a bowl of noodles that has the markings of being handmade: a variety of strands—some thick, some thin—with ends where you can see where they've been pulled apart. These noodles are made to be thrown into a simmering pot of soup or boiled and then stir fried in a delicious sauce.

2 cups "00" flour or all-purpose flour, plus more for dusting

¼ teaspoon kosher salt

¾ cup water

Grapeseed oil or vegetable oil

Makes 1 pound

MAKE THE DOUGH: Mix the flour and salt together in a medium mixing bowl. Gently pour the water into the mixing bowl, incorporating it into the flour with a silicone spatula until loosely combined. Transfer to a lightly floured work surface and knead until smooth like a baby's butt, about 10 minutes. Let it rest for 15 minutes, then roll into a thick cylinder and cut into six equal pieces. With your fingers, flatten each piece until it resembles an oval that's 2 by 4 inches long. Oil each piece of dough and set onto a plate or tray covered with plastic wrap to rest again for another hour.

PULL THE NOODLES: Set a piece of rested dough onto a large flat working surface. With a chopstick, press into the middle of the dough lengthwise to create a recessed line. With your hands, grab each short end of the dough and gently pull to stretch and lengthen the dough. Start swinging the dough up and down, slapping the work surface with the dough as you slowly pull the noodles wider. Once you've pulled to reach chest length, locate the halfway point of the noodle and pull the two halves apart to create two strands of noodles. Dust the noodles with a generous sprinkling of flour, then repeat with the remaining dough pieces. Cook immediately, or store in an airtight container in the freezer for up to 6 months.

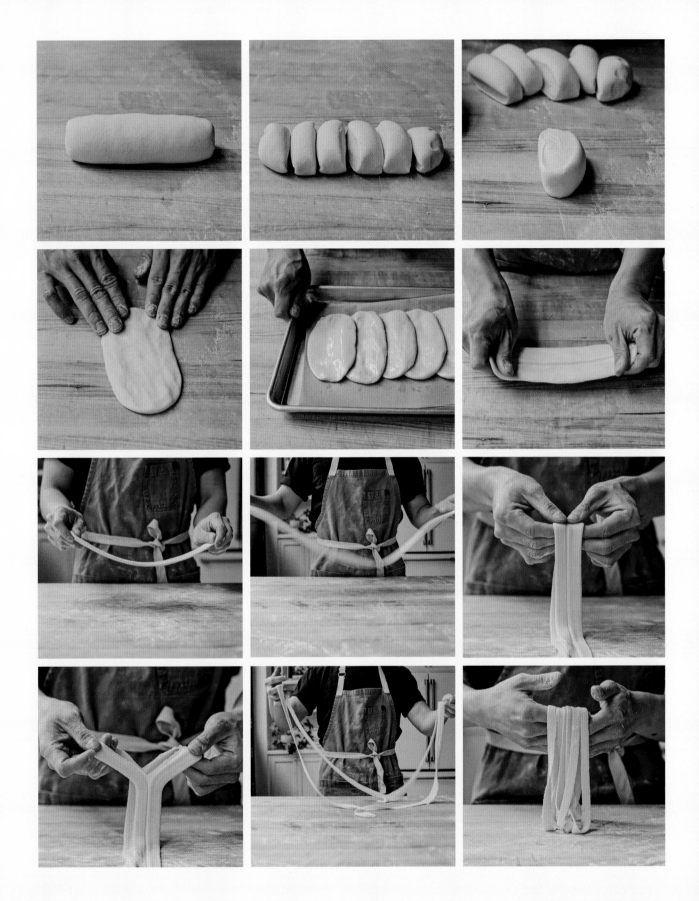

As my parents worked longer hours, my grandma moved in with us: a familiar rite of passage for many Asian immigrant families with working parents. A curious cold noodle dish called liang mian began showing up on the counter when I came home from school. My grandma told me it was a common everyday meal she would have during Taiwan summers, accessible at a cheap price at street stands. I had never seen a noodle slathered in peanut butter, a flavor I associated mostly with my favorite Reese's Cups and peanut-butter-and-jelly sandwiches. Raw green cucumber slices sat right next to this peanut sauce, along with what looked like chopped scrambled egg. I hesitantly took one bite. It was definitely peanut butter, but its punches of soy sauce, garlic, and ginger tapped into another realm of savory flavor that made me want more. A second bite, with fresh cucumber and salty scrambled egg, made me a convert. The combination of chewy with crunchy and salty with sweet was delightfully refreshing, especially on a hot afternoon. I haven't stopped eating this dish since. This recipe uses instant ramen, mostly for nostalgia's sake. Our family loved the texture of instant ramen, its distinct chewiness still a staple of my pantry today; it's also a noodle that delivers on value and efficiency. The toppings are made to be played with; try adding different ingredients like julienned raw carrots, celery, or mung bean sprouts to make the dish all your own.

COLD RAMEN NOODLE SALAD WITH GINGER AND GARLIC PEANUT SAUCE

PREP THE EGGS: In a nonstick skillet over medium heat, warm the oil. Add the eggs and swirl the skillet to create an even layer of egg. Cook until the bottom of the egg becomes firm, then flip and cook the other side until it's cooked through. Remove from the pan and cut into three even slices. Stack the slices on top of each other and cut across into thin strips.

MAKE THE SAUCE: In a medium mixing bowl, combine the peanut butter, water, soy sauce, ginger, garlic, honey, and salt, and whisk until smooth. Set aside.

MAKE THE NOODLES AND ASSEMBLE: Cook the instant ramen according to package directions until it has just reached al dente. Drain the noodles, then rinse with cold water and drain again. Add the noodles to the mixing bowl with the sauce and toss to combine. Divide the noodles among two bowls and top with the sliced egg, cucumber, scallions, and cilantro. Sprinkle with sesame seeds and red pepper flakes, and serve.

EGGS

1 tablespoon canola oil or vegetable oil

2 eggs, beaten

PEANUT SAUCE

3 tablespoons creamy peanut butter

4 tablespoons warm water

2 tablespoons soy sauce

1 teaspoon grated fresh ginger

1 teaspoon grated garlic (about 3 cloves)

1 tablespoon honey

1/2 teaspoon kosher salt

NOODLES

2 packages instant ramen

TOPPINGS

Julienned English cucumber

Chopped scallions

Chopped cilantro

White sesame seeds

Red pepper flakes

Makes 2 servings

SCALLION MAC AND "CHEESE"

My love of Olive Garden knows no bounds. A restaurant worthy of its iconic suburban status, its endless breadsticks, Zuppa Toscana, and all-you-can-eat salad rivals the excitement I feel eating at a Michelin-star restaurant. If there's one dish you must order at Olive Garden, it's the macaroni and cheese from the kids menu—a perfectly al dente shell pasta coated in light, buttery creaminess that I still look forward to every visit. I dreamed up this recipe after romanticizing about a world in which my grandma and I could do an Olive Garden pop-up in the restaurant's kitchen. This recipe, a creamy mac and cheese with layers of scallion flavor embedded into the sauce, would be my contribution. The sauce is cashew-based, as many of my relatives are lactose intolerant (a genetic travesty no one should have to go through). However, that intolerance has resulted in this dish, which is completely dairy-free yet just as light and creamy as the Olive Garden original. Scallions are pan-fried and then blended directly into the sauce, adding the perfect aromatic complement to balance out the "cheese."

SCALLION CASHEW CHEESE

2 cups raw unsalted cashews

1/4 cup olive oil

8 scallions, green and white parts, chopped

4 garlic cloves, smashed

3 teaspoons kosher salt

1 teaspoon granulated sugar

1/4 teaspoon sweet paprika

Juice of 1/2 lemon

1 cup water

TOPPINGS

1/2 cup panko

2 scallions, green and white parts

NOODLES

1 pound dried macaroni

Makes 4 servings

PREP THE CASHEWS: A few hours before cooking, pour the cashews into a medium mixing bowl and cover with water by 1 inch. Soak for 2 to 3 hours. Strain and set aside.

MAKE THE SCALLION CASHEW CHEESE: In a medium skillet over medium-high heat, warm the olive oil. Add the scallions and garlic; the oil should start sizzling. Stir and cook for 2 minutes, until the scallions have softened slightly and the oil is fragrant. Transfer to a blender and add the soaked cashews, salt, sugar, paprika, lemon juice, and water. Blend until smooth. Taste and adjust the salt or acid as needed, then set aside.

PREP THE TOPPINGS: To the same skillet that was used to fry the scallions and garlic, add the panko and cook for a few minutes on low-medium heat, stirring, until it's golden brown. Set aside. Chop the scallions and set aside.

COOK THE MACARONI: Bring a large pot of salted water to a boil. Add the macaroni to the pot and cook until just al dente, according to the package instructions. Drain the macaroni, then return it to the pot.

ASSEMBLE THE MACARONI: Add the blended cashew cheese to the pot of macaroni and stir to combine. Turn the heat to medium and cook for a couple minutes, stirring occasionally, to warm everything up. Divide the mac and cheese among four serving bowls and top with a sprinkling of toasted panko and chopped scallions. Serve immediately.

STIR-FRIED RICE CAKES WITH BOK CHOY AND SHIITAKE MUSHROOMS

炒年糕

Asian rice cakes are a satisfyingly chewy noodle made of glutinous rice flour. Rice cakes serve as a neutral base ready to absorb flavor, taking on a coating of sauce in a stir-fry like a sponge. When we wanted to relive memories of eating at our favorite Taiwanese restaurant, Din Tai Fung, this dish found a place at our dinner table. Though many families enjoy it year-round, this Shanghainese recipe is historically associated with celebrating the Chinese New Year.

RICE CAKES

1 pound rice cakes

SAUCE

3/4 cup chicken stock

1/2 teaspoon soy sauce

1/2 teaspoon kosher salt

1/4 teaspoon granulated sugar

1/4 teaspoon grated fresh ginger

STIR-FRY

Vegetable oil

2 scallions, green and white parts, chopped

2 garlic cloves, sliced

2 medium carrots, thinly sliced

2 cups sliced shiitake mushrooms

1 baby bok choy, base trimmed and leaves pulled apart

TOPPINGS

Chopped scallions

Chopped roasted, unsalted peanuts

Kosher salt

Makes 3 servings

PREP THE RICE CAKES: Place the rice cakes in a large bowl and cover with water by 1 inch. Let soak at room temperature for 2 hours, or in the fridge, covered, up to overnight. Drain and set aside.

MAKE THE SAUCE: In a small mixing bowl, stir together the chicken stock, soy sauce, salt, sugar, and ginger. Set aside.

STIR-FRY AND SERVE: In a large skillet over medium heat, warm 1 tablespoon oil. Add the scallions and garlic and sauté until fragrant, about 30 seconds. Add the carrots and continuously stir and sauté until easily pierced through with a knife, about 5 minutes. Add the mushrooms and cook for another 2 to 3 minutes, until the mushrooms have softened. Pour in the sauce and add the drained rice cakes and the bok choy. Stir continuously until the rice cakes have softened and are cooked through, 2 to 3 minutes. Remove from the heat, divide among three bowls, and top with scallions, peanuts, and a sprinkle of salt to serve.

Zhajiangmian, a bowl of noodles I only encountered when visiting my grandma in Memphis, always reminds me of early childhood. Originating in northern China, it's a classic recipe with many variations across regions, its flavors evolving as it made its way to places such as Korea (where it became jajangmyeon) and Japan (where it became jajamen). It's made with sweet bean sauce, also known in Chinese as tian mian jiang (甜面酱). The English translation is deceiving because although there are soybeans in the sauce, it's primarily made with fermented wheat flour, which creates its signature sweet umami flavor. The sweet bean sauce is simmered with ground pork and aromatics to create a complex meat sauce almost like a Bolognese. It's poured over fresh noodles then topped with sliced cucumbers and herbs for a refreshing bite that balances the depth of the sauce.

HAND-CUT NOODLES WITH MINCED PORK SAUCE

炸醬麵

(Zhá Jiàng Miàn)

PREP THE MEAT MIXTURE FOR THE SAUCE: In a medium mixing bowl, cover the mushrooms with 1 inch of water and let soak at room temperature for about 30 minutes, until soft. Remove the mushrooms, reserving the soaking water, and finely dice. In a large mixing bowl, combine the ground pork, mushrooms, scallions, ginger, and garlic with your hands until the mixture feels sticky. Set aside.

MAKE THE SAUCE: In a large saucepan over medium-high heat, warm 1 tablespoon oil. Add the shallots and cook until they start to become transparent, 3 to 4 minutes. Add the meat mixture and cook, stirring occasionally, until it has browned and cooked through. Once the pork is browned, pour the sake into the pan and let it boil until the alcohol has cooked off, 20 to 30 seconds. Turn the heat down to medium. Measure out 1 cup of the mushroom soaking water and add it to the pan along with the almond soy glaze, sweet bean sauce, and salt. Stir and simmer until the sauce starts to thicken and is the consistency of pasta sauce, 10 to 15 minutes. If the sauce becomes too thick, add more mushroom water by the tablespoon to thin it out. Once the sauce is done, set aside.

COOK THE NOODLES AND ASSEMBLE: Bring a large pot of salted water to a boil. Add the noodles and cook to al dente, 1 to 2 minutes for homemade noodles or according to package directions if using store-bought. Drain the noodles and transfer to a large mixing bowl. Pour your desired amount of sauce over the noodles (you might not use all the sauce) and mix with tongs until all the noodles are coated. Divide the noodles among four bowls and garnish with cucumber, radishes, scallions, and cilantro. Serve immediately.

SAUCE

⅓ cup dried shiitake mushrooms

½ pound ground pork

2 scallions, green and white parts, finely chopped

1 teaspoon grated fresh ginger

3 garlic cloves, grated

Canola oil or vegetable oil

3 shallots, finely diced

¼ cup sake

⅓ cup Almond Soy Glaze (page 11)

¼ cup sweet bean sauce (甜面酱)

½ teaspoon kosher salt

NOODLES

1 recipe Flour Noodles (page 84) or Egg Noodles (page 87), or 1 pound store-bought fresh or dried noodles

TOPPINGS

Julienned English cucumber

Thinly sliced radishes

Chopped scallions

Chopped cilantro

Makes 4 servings

NOODLES AND RICE

One could say that this is the national dish of Taiwan—a bowl synonymous with pride for a nation of Taiwanese families and the generations of Taiwanese immigrants who've come from them. The perfect bowl of beef noodle soup doesn't exist at one specific place or come from one specific recipe. Whether it's the neighborhood spot near a childhood apartment in Taipei or a glistening bowl from Yongkang Street, the perfect noodle soup is simply the one that conjures a sense of satisfying nostalgia in the moment. I grew up with my Uncle Jerry's beef noodle soup, from which this recipe is adapted. It's a dish his mother made for him and in turn he made it for me. Its tender braised beef sits alongside strands of chewy noodles. The broth has a deeply concentrated beef flavor that pairs well with the acidity of tomato and the sweetness of onion. For me, it's a familiar comfort with every hearty spoonful (and loud slurp).

TAIWANESE BEEF NOODLE SOUP

紅燒牛肉麵

BROWN THE MEAT: Place a large pot or Dutch oven over medium-high heat and add a generous pour of oil. When the oil is hot, add the beef and brown on all sides. Remove the beef, set aside, and turn the heat down to medium.

COOK THE BROTH AND BEEF: Add 1 to 2 tablespoons oil to the pot and add the onions, scallions, tomatoes, and garlic. Sauté until the onions are semitranslucent, stirring occasionally so the onions don't burn, about 5 minutes.

Return the browned beef to the pot. Stir in the Shaoxing wine, soy sauce, brown sugar, cinnamon, star anise, orange zest, cloves, and ginger. Add water until it reaches a little bit above all the ingredients (about 5 cups). Bring the mixture to a boil, then lower the heat so it's gently simmering. Cover with a lid but leave a little gap to let the steam escape. Simmer for 2 to 2½ hours, until the beef is cooked through and tender.

COOK THE NOODLES AND ASSEMBLE: When the soup is just about ready, remove the cinnamon stick, star anise, and orange zest and discard. Fish out the beef chunks and cut them into smaller pieces, then place them back into the pot and let them soak in more flavor as the broth finishes cooking.

Meanwhile, bring a large pot of generously salted water to a boil. Add in the whole bok choy and boil until tender but retaining some crispness, about 4 minutes. Fish out the bok choy with tongs, cut each one in half lengthwise, and set aside. To the same boiling water, add the noodles and cook until just al dente, about 1 minute if using homemade noodles or according to package instructions if using store-bought. Drain the noodles and evenly divide among serving bowls. Add one to two bok choy halves to each bowl. Taste the soup and season with salt if needed. Ladle the hot soup into the serving bowls, making sure to get beef in each serving, and sprinkle with scallions and cilantro. Serve immediately.

BEEF

Canola oil or vegetable oil

2 pounds beef shanks, cut into 2 or 3 pieces

BROTH

Canola oil or vegetable oil

2 yellow onions, diced

3 scallions, green and white parts, chopped

2 medium tomatoes, roughly chopped

4 garlic cloves, sliced

1 cup Shaoxing wine

¼ cup soy sauce

1 tablespoon light brown sugar

1 cinnamon stick

1 star anise pod

1 three-inch-long strip orange zest

5 whole cloves

4 thumb-sized slices ginger

NOODLES AND TOPPINGS

4 baby bok choy

Double recipe Flour Noodles (page 84), or 2 pounds store-bought fresh or dried noodles

Kosher salt (optional)

Chopped scallions

Chopped cilantro

Makes 4 to 6 servings

STIR-FRIED RICE CAKE BOLOGNESE

I can trace my love of Bolognese all the way back to third grade, when my best friend, who lived across the street, introduced me to what would become one of my favorite meals: SpaghettiOs with Meatballs. As a spaghetti enthusiast, a trail of canned tomato and meat sauces has come along with me ever since, until I eventually reached a destination and found the recipes of Marcella Hazan. A first-generation Italian American immigrant, Hazan can be credited with shaping a generation of Americans' definitions of Italian food. Cooking her Bolognese recipe for the first time, I discovered pure bliss, an expression of beef and tomato completely transformed after a "lazy simmer," as she liked to say. Curiously, tasting Hazan's Bolognese brought me not to Italy but to my own Taiwanese grandma and her fragrant simmered pork sauces poured over fresh noodles or rice. This recipe highlights the commonalities between different cultures. Rice cakes serve as the chewy base for a Bolognese sauce inspired by Hazan, while mixing in ingredients that are love letters to both Italian and Taiwanese tradition.

RICE CAKES

24 ounces rice cakes

BOLOGNESE

Olive oil

2 yellow onions, diced

2 medium carrots, diced

2 celery stalks, diced

2 scallions, green and white parts, chopped

1 teaspoon minced garlic (1 large clove)

1 teaspoon minced fresh ginger

1/2 pound 80/20 ground beef

1/2 pound ground pork

1 cup whole milk

1 whole nutmeg

1 cup white wine

1/2 cinnamon stick

2 bay leaves

2 tablespoons soy sauce

One 28-ounce can crushed tomatoes with juice

Freshly ground black pepper

TOPPINGS

Grated Parmesan cheese

Torn basil leaves

Makes 4 servings

PREP THE RICE CAKES: Place the rice cakes in a large bowl and cover with water by 1 inch. Let soak at room temperature for 2 hours, or in the fridge, covered, up to overnight. Drain and set aside.

MAKE THE BOLOGNESE: In a large pot over medium heat, warm a generous glug of olive oil. Add the onions, carrots, celery, scallions, garlic, and ginger, and cook until the onions are semitranslucent, about 5 minutes.

Add the ground beef and pork to the pot and cook, stirring and breaking up the chunks of meat, until the beef has browned, about 7 minutes.

Stir in the milk and let it simmer until it has evaporated. Using a nutmeg grater or other fine grater, grate 8 zips of nutmeg into the pot. Stir in the white wine and simmer until it has mostly evaporated. Add the cinnamon stick, bay leaves, soy sauce, and tomatoes and increase the heat to bring everything to a light boil, then reduce the heat until it is very gently simmering, where just a burp of a bubble breaks the surface intermittently. Cook, uncovered, for 3 hours, until thickened.

ASSEMBLE THE DISH: Transfer the Bolognese to a large saucepan, add the rice cakes, and stir-fry for a few minutes, until the rice cakes are soft and cooked through. Divide among four bowls, sprinkle with a light flurry of Parmesan and fresh basil, and serve.

Cincinnati-style chili, pioneered by the restaurant Skyline Chili, is the quintessential dish of the city I grew up in. I would describe it as a sauce rather than a chili, its warm spices of cumin, cinnamon, and chili powder giving it an aromatic depth similar to that of a Mexican mole or a Taiwanese minced-meat sauce. This recipe is inspired by my favorite order at Skyline, known as the "4-Way": noodles topped with a generous portion of their signature chili, freshly diced onions, and a heaping pile of cheese. I aim to borrow from Skyline Chili, using many of the same rich spices in their recipe while adapting it to be the perfect companion to homemade noodles and fresh scallions.

CINCINNATI CHILI WITH FLOUR NOODLES

MAKE THE CINCINNATI CHILI: In a large pot over medium heat, warm the olive oil. Add the onions and cook, stirring often, until translucent, about 5 minutes. Add the garlic and ground beef and continue to cook, stirring occasionally, until the beef has changed from red to light brown in color. Add the red pepper flakes, cumin, salt, allspice, chili powder, and cinnamon, and sauté to incorporate. Add the tomato sauce, vinegar, Worcestershire, chocolate, and bay leaf. Pour in the water and mix everything together. Bring to a boil, then simmer on low heat, uncovered, for 45 minutes to 1 hour, stirring occasionally so the chili doesn't stick to the bottom.

MAKE THE NOODLES: Cook the flour noodles as directed (on page 84), or according to package directions if you're using store-bought noodles. Drain and set aside.

ASSEMBLE THE DISH: When the chili is done, remove the bay leaf. Taste and adjust the seasonings. Divide the noodles among four bowls and top each with a heaping scoop of chili. Garnish with a sprinkling of Parmesan cheese and scallions, and serve immediately.

CHILI

1 tablespoon olive oil

1 medium yellow onion, diced

2 garlic cloves, grated

1 pound 80/20 ground beef

½ teaspoon red pepper flakes

1 teaspoon ground cumin

2 teaspoons kosher salt

½ teaspoon ground allspice

1 tablespoon chili powder

1 teaspoon ground cinnamon

One 8-ounce can tomato sauce

2 tablespoons white vinegar

2 teaspoons Worcestershire sauce

1 ounce unsweetened chocolate, chopped

1 large bay leaf

3 cups water

NOODLES

1 recipe Hand-Pulled Noodles (page 88)

TOPPINGS

Grated Parmesan cheese

Chopped scallions

Makes 4 servings

WHITE RICE

A staple among every Asian family, probably second only to oxygen (with water a distant third). I typically cook white rice in a rice cooker with a 1-to-1 ratio of rice to water; it's a foolproof way to steam perfectly cooked rice with a press of a button. Before writing this book, I'd never cooked rice on a stovetop. However, I've learned to embrace the stove when a rice cooker isn't on hand; I use this method, which results in fluffy grains of rice.

1 tablespoon canola oil or vegetable oil

1½ cups water

1 cup medium-grain white rice

Makes about 3 cups

In a medium saucepan over medium heat, warm the oil. Pour in the rice and stir until the grains become coated in oil, a few minutes or so. Add the water and bring to a boil. Turn the heat down to low and give the rice one last mix to dislodge any grains on the bottom. Cover and simmer for 15 to 20 minutes without touching it. Once the rice absorbed all the water, remove it from the heat and let it continue to steam, still covered, for 10 minutes. Fluff with a fork and serve.

Tip:
Use store-bought or homemade stock like Chicken Stock (page 12) or Simple Vegetable Stock (page 13) instead of water to enhance the flavor of the rice from the inside. When it's cooked, sprinkle with a little salt and furikake and it becomes a delicious side all on its own.

A satisfyingly sticky grain that is the base for many classic rice dishes, like fan tuan (a Taiwanese breakfast staple of youtiao and pork floss wrapped in sticky rice; page 46) and youfan (a steamed sticky rice dish made with soy sauce and shiitake mushroom). Sticky rice can be cooked in many ways, but this particular method, which steams the rice to a perfectly soft and chewy texture, only requires a steamer, boiling water, and some cloth.

STICKY RICE

The night before, place the glutinous rice in a medium mixing bowl. Add water to cover by 1 inch and place in the fridge to soak overnight.

The following day, drain the rice. Fill a pot that will fit a bamboo or metal steamer with an inch of water and bring to a boil. Wet a thin cotton cloth or piece of muslin or cheesecloth that is large enough to line the steamer and have some overhang. Place the rice onto the wet cloth and wrap the excess cloth around the rice like a package. Place the lid on the steamer and place the steamer in the pot (or place the steamer in the pot and then put the lid on the pot). Turn the heat to medium-high and steam for 25 to 30 minutes, until the grains have completely softened.

2 cups sweet glutinous rice

Makes 4 cups

STIR-FRIED TOMATOES AND EGGS WITH WHITE RICE

蕃茄炒蛋

This simple homestyle dish is scrambled eggs in a savory-sweet stir-fried tomato sauce that's been cooked down with scallions and ginger. Its unassuming tastiness hides the profound impact this recipe has had on so many Chinese and Taiwanese American immigrants and the generations that have followed them. A simple spoonful of stir-fried tomato egg with white rice has the ability to completely transport someone to their family and roots. This was a dish my dad made for me when I was growing up, and something he made when he craved home after immigrating to America. It was a standby at all our family meals, as ever-present on the table as a steamer of rice or a glass of water. A dish that today still conjures for me the same overwhelming cravings of memory and nostalgia for the home I grew up in, just like it did for my dad.

6 eggs

1 tablespoon chicken stock

½ teaspoon toasted sesame oil

1½ teaspoons kosher salt

4 tablespoons vegetable oil

4 scallions, green and white parts, chopped, plus extra for garnish

½ teaspoon grated fresh ginger

1 teaspoon grated garlic (about 3 cloves)

¾ pound tomatoes (about 2 large beefsteak), cut into 1-inch wedges

½ teaspoon granulated sugar

2 tablespoons ketchup

1 recipe White Rice (page 102)

Makes 2 servings

PREP THE EGGS: In a medium mixing bowl, beat the eggs with the chicken stock, sesame oil, and ½ teaspoon of the salt.

COOK THE EGGS: In a medium saucepan over high heat, warm 2 tablespoons of the vegetable oil. When the oil is just about to smoke, carefully add the eggs and stir continuously until they firm up, 30 to 45 seconds. Return the eggs to the mixing bowl, then wipe out the pan.

In the same pan, warm the remaining 2 tablespoons vegetable oil over medium-high heat. Add the scallions, ginger, and garlic and stir constantly until fragrant, about 10 seconds. Add the tomatoes and continue to cook, stirring occasionally, for 2 to 3 minutes, until the tomatoes have started to break down a bit and their juices start to simmer.

Turn the heat down to low and add the remaining 1 teaspoon salt, the sugar, and the ketchup. Mix until fully incorporated, then return the eggs to the pan, stirring to fold them into the sauce. Serve the tomato eggs topped with some chopped scallions and a bowl of rice alongside.

There's magic to food that stems from adversity—recipes that use simple ingredients, time, and ingenuity to transform into something that's undeniably delicious. Congee was historically a peasant food, a way for the poor to stretch supplies of rice and have more rations for meals. Its ability to nurture has led it to become a staple comfort food in Asian households today. This congee is adapted from a recipe from one of my best friends, Kelly, who still craves congee even though her family has lived in America for five generations. In this recipe, rice and chicken drumsticks cook in a simmering water broth, the water and rice slowly taking on the flavor of the bones. Blanching the meat first is a method commonly used to take out impurities, which results in a clearer broth. Chicken or turkey bones can also be used to make the broth, without the blanching step.

LAU-KEE CONGEE

Place the drumsticks in a large pot. Add cold water to cover by 1 inch. Bring to a boil and cook until scum floats to the top. Remove the pot from the heat and pour out the dirty water. Rinse the meat with warm water and drain, then return to the pot. (If using chicken or turkey bones to make the broth, simply place the bones in a large pot.)

Pour 2½ quarts of fresh water into the pot and add the rice, daikon, scallions, and ginger. Bring to a boil, then lower to a slow simmer. Cook for 1½ to 2 hours, making sure to stir every 20 minutes or so to avoid the rice burning on the bottom, until the congee has thickened to an oatmeal-like consistency. Remove any meat from the bones and discard the bones. Add salt to taste. Ladle into bowls, top with scallions and a drizzle of soy sauce, and serve immediately.

2½ pounds chicken drumsticks, chicken bones, or turkey bones

¾ cup medium-grain white rice

1 medium daikon or turnip, sliced thick

2 scallions, green and white parts, chopped, plus extra for garnish

2 thumb-sized slices ginger

Kosher salt

Soy sauce for serving

Makes 6 servings

FRIED EGG RICE WITH CILANTRO

There's something about Chipotle's cilantro rice that my dad and I could never get enough of. We always ordered their burrito bowls with extra rice, giving the server the stink eye until the bowl was filled to our satisfaction. My dad also used to make me simple two-ingredient rice bowls at home—white rice with a scrambled egg and a little salt. It was a basic bowl yet perfectly dialed in for homey warmth, as satisfying to me as a Michelin two-star meal (not that I'm biased or anything). The love for rice that my dad and I shared, plus memories of our trips to Chipotle, combined to create this recipe. It's a simple bed of white-rice nostalgia mixed with just three other ingredients: lime juice, a generous sprinkling of herbaceous cilantro, and soft scrambled egg. It's essentially egg fried rice, the brightness of lime singing through while chunks of egg add a familiar comfort.

3 tablespoons
vegetable oil

1 cup medium-grain
white rice

2 cups Chicken
Stock (see page 12)
or water

Kosher salt

Juice of ½ lime

1 tablespoon
chopped cilantro

3 eggs

Chopped scallions
for serving

Black sesame seeds
for serving

Makes 2 servings

SIMMER THE RICE: In a large nonstick shallow pan or pot with a lid, warm 1 tablespoon of the oil over medium heat. Add the rice and cook, stirring, until the rice grains become translucent, about 5 minutes. Add the chicken stock or water and bring to a boil. Reduce the heat to low and let the rice simmer, covered, for 15 to 20 minutes, without touching it.

MAKE THE LIME AND SALT MIXTURE: While the rice simmers, in a small mixing bowl, stir together ¾ teaspoon salt and the lime juice until the salt dissolves. Set aside.

STEAM THE RICE: Once the rice has absorbed all the water, remove it from the heat and let it continue to steam, covered, for 10 minutes. Fluff with a fork. Add the lime-salt mixture and the cilantro, and mix until incorporated.

COOK THE EGGS AND ASSEMBLE THE DISH: In a small mixing bowl, beat the eggs with a sprinkle of salt and set aside. In a small skillet over high heat, warm the remaining 2 tablespoons oil until shimmering. Carefully pour the beaten eggs into the skillet; they'll start to bubble a lot as they fry in the hot oil. With a spatula, move the egg around in the pan until it's scrambled, 30 seconds to 1 minute. Remove from the heat and add to the cilantro-lime rice. With a fork, mix everything together. Divide among two bowls, garnish with scallions and sesame seeds, and serve immediately.

This homestyle broth of baby back ribs simmered alongside carrots and daikon was a mainstay in my family's kitchen; a meal never went by without a bowl of light broth to hydrate and nourish. My mom always made sure my serving of soup had the meatiest ribs, while I always added a spoonful of rice to soak up all the broth's flavor and make the dish heartier.

BLANCH THE RIBS: Fill a large pot with cold water and add the ribs. Bring to a boil and cook until scum rises to the top of the water, about 5 minutes. Fish out the ribs with tongs and pour out the dirty water. Give the ribs a good rinse with hot water and drain. Pat the ribs dry with paper towels.

BROWN THE RIBS AND SIMMER THE STOCK: In a large saucepan over medium-high heat, warm a generous glug of oil. Add the ribs and lightly brown to seal in flavor. In a large, clean pot, combine the ribs, carrots, daikon, corn, scallions, and ginger, and add water to just cover the ingredients. Bring to a boil, then reduce the heat and simmer for 45 minutes. In the last 10 minutes, taste the soup. If it needs salt, season with a sprinkle of salt. If it needs acid, add a dash of black vinegar.

ASSEMBLE THE DISH: Scoop a few spoonfuls of rice into each of the four serving bowls, then divide the broth among the bowls, pouring it over the rice. Make sure each bowl has ribs, carrots, and daikon. Sprinkle with scallions and cilantro, and serve immediately.

PORK BONE BROTH WITH RICE

排骨湯

3 pounds pork baby back ribs or spare ribs, cut in pieces

Canola oil or vegetable oil

3 medium carrots, peeled and coarsely chopped

2 daikon, peeled and coarsely chopped

1 ear corn, husked and cut in half horizontally

4 scallions, green and white parts, chopped

3 thumb-sized slices ginger

Kosher salt (optional)

Black vinegar (optional)

1 recipe White Rice (page 102)

Chopped scallions for garnish

Chopped cilantro for garnish

Makes 4 servings

LU ROU FAN

Lu rou fan is a homey dish that's beloved in Taiwan, and perhaps just as iconic as Taiwanese beef noodle soup. It's a bowl of comfort: diced pork belly and shiitake mushrooms are braised in soy sauce and Shaoxing wine to create a fatty, lick-your-lips meat sauce destined to be eaten over white rice. Every salty bite is an indulgence, the shiny sauce glistening with pork fat coating fragrant tender meat as it dribbles over each grain of rice.

1 cup dried shiitake mushrooms

SPICE PACKET

1 three-inch-long strip orange zest

3 thumb-sized slices of ginger

1 cinnamon stick

2 bay leaves

3 star anise pods

2 whole cloves

MEAT SAUCE

Canola oil or vegetable oil

3 shallots, diced

1 pound pork belly, diced

¼ cup soy sauce

¼ cup Shaoxing wine

2½ teaspoons light brown sugar

2 cups cooked white rice (page 102)

4 Soft-Boiled Tea Eggs (page 24), optional

Chopped cilantro for garnish

Makes 4 servings

PREP THE MUSHROOMS: In a medium mixing bowl, cover the mushrooms with 3 cups of water. Set aside to soak, at least 30 minutes and up to 1 hour. Drain, reserving 2 cups of the soaking water. Dice the mushrooms and set aside.

MAKE THE SPICE PACKET: Place the orange peel, ginger, cinnamon stick, bay leaves, star anise, and cloves on a large piece of cheesecloth and tie the ends together with a piece of string.

MAKE THE MEAT SAUCE: In a large pot over medium heat, warm a generous glug of oil. Add the shallots and sauté until translucent and softened, about 2 minutes. Add the pork belly and stir-fry until the pork has browned a bit in color. Add the diced mushrooms and stir-fry for about 1 minute. Add the reserved 2 cups mushroom soaking water, the soy sauce, Shaoxing wine, brown sugar, and the spice packet, and stir to combine.

Bring the sauce to a boil, then lower the heat and let it gently simmer for 1 to 1½ hours, stirring occasionally, until the pork is tender and the sauce has thickened. When the sauce is done, remove the spice packet. Divide the rice among four bowls and and spoon the meat sauce over. Top with a halved egg, if using, and sprinkle with cilantro. Serve immediately.

Fried rice is a delicious game of leftovers. Growing up, this fried rice recipe was the particular combination of ingredients I happened to love most. Every bite is filled with a burst of textures and flavors that bring me back to my childhood. The hearty chew of chicken thigh provides meatiness and a satisfying mouthfeel. The light sweetness of carrots balances out the Spam's salty fattiness. Cilantro and romaine lettuce provide a pop of freshness in between slippery grains of rice. All these seemingly disparate ingredients somehow feel meant to be together. This recipe calls for fresh rice but leftover works as well.

CHILDHOOD FRIED RICE

In a small mixing bowl, beat the eggs. Place the scallions, cilantro, Spam, and chicken into separate bowls. In a large wok or nonstick pan, heat a generous amount of oil over high heat until it's just smoking. Add half the scallions and half the cilantro to the oil, then add the beaten egg. Continuously stir the egg until it firms up, 10 to 20 seconds. Transfer the eggs to a bowl and set aside. Wipe out the pan and add a generous amount of oil. Return the pan to high heat. Add the Spam and chicken and a pinch each of salt and sugar. Stir-fry until the chicken has cooked through, about 5 minutes. Add the carrots and stir-fry for about 2 minutes, until the carrots have softened. Add the rice, 1 teaspoon salt, and ¾ teaspoon sugar. Toss lightly to evenly mix. Turn the heat off and add the scrambled eggs and the remaining scallions and cilantro. Lightly mix to incorporate all the ingredients, then divide among three bowls and serve immediately.

3 eggs

4 scallions, green and white parts, finely chopped

1 cup chopped cilantro

1 cup finely chopped Spam

½ pound boneless, skinless chicken thighs, finely chopped

Canola oil or vegetable oil (or any neutral oil)

Kosher salt

Granulated sugar

2 medium carrots, finely chopped

1 recipe White Rice (page 102)

Makes 3 servings

DUMPLING

05

S AND BAO

Twinkie

"White on the inside, yellow on the outside" was my teenage version of "keys, cell phone, wallet" every time I walked out the door. I thrived on being called a "Twinkie," a merit badge well earned through extensive R&D that included everything from purchases at American Eagle to absorbing every pop-culture morsel of teen angst on MTV's *Laguna Beach*. To be called a Twinkie by my predominantly white classmates meant I did my job to fit in, and that I could perhaps even thrive despite my jet-black hair and Asian features. I told myself I was never going to be one of *those* Asians, the ones that got sidelined for having even the slightest accent or, God forbid, brought their family's homemade dumplings for a cafeteria full of moody hormonal teenagers to see and smell. Nope, I was going to be the whitest, creamiest Twinkie these damn kids had ever seen. And yet, no matter how hard I tried to separate my two worlds, burying an Asian immigrant family's home life on one side while projecting an all-American kid on the other, the food my family cooked made it difficult to sever a connection to my roots. Particularly when those roots happened to be the birthplace of two of the world's most undeniably delicious inventions: steamed bao and dumplings. I spent so much of my childhood trying to pretend I wasn't anything like my parents, and yet the sight of a bamboo steamer fresh off the stove and my overwhelming appetite unwittingly pulled me back to the Taiwanese identity that I had buried deep within myself. Every bite of my grandma's lovingly handmade bao transported me to the humid, cramped kitchens my parents grew up in or to the bustling street markets of Taipei they'd told me stories about: places I'd never been yet felt surprisingly familiar.

As I've grown into adulthood, my self-doubt has slowly drifted away. These dumplings and bao recipes are a celebration of owning an identity that exists in the in-between, where delicious food can point to a distinct Asian American experience. They reference a conversation across traditions and cultures. My upbringing in the Midwest is pork shumai in creamy corn broth (page 150). My grandma's home in Memphis is gua bao filled with black vinegar barbecue brisket (page 161). And, if I could go back in time, the dumplings I'd now proudly stuff my face in front of all those kids in the cafeteria are pork and cabbage dumplings (page 138).

As I sit here eating a steamed bao with one hand and typing with the other, I can't help but laugh at how insecure the younger Frankie was, and how much his dumplings and culture brought him so much shame—when in fact they were his superpower. If only he knew that those very dumplings would be the reason he'd be able to publish this book. If only he knew that he'd be able to tell immigrant kids just like him that their identities and stories should be celebrated, because those identities and stories are what make them distinctly American. It is their unique existence in this country that makes America thrive.

Dumpling & Bao Doughs

Dumpling Terms

PAN-FRIED DUMPLING
Guōtiē 鍋貼

A filled dumpling that's pan-fried to achieve its distinct crispy bottom

BOILED DUMPLING
Shuǐjiǎo 水餃

A filled dumpling that's boiled in water

SHUMAI
燒賣

A filled dumpling with an open top

Bao Terms

BAO OR BAOZI
包子

A delightfully fluffy steamed bun that's filled with meat and/or vegetables

PAN-FRIED BUN
Shuǐ jiān bāo 水煎包

A steamed bun that's pan-fried and simmered in shallow water to achieve its distinct crispy bottom while retaining its fluffy texture

GUA BAO
刈包

An open-faced steamed bun in the form of a clamshell that traditionally holds pork belly, pickled mustard greens, ground peanuts, and cilantro

DUMPLING WRAPPERS

This classic chewy dumpling wrapper lends itself well to steaming, pan-frying, or boiling. I love making thicker wrappers when boiling dumplings, as the wrapper holds up well to a boil and results in a chewy, QQ texture. For steaming, I make thinner wrappers, as they retain less moisture during the delicate cooking process. When it comes to pan frying, I'm pretty loose with the thickness of the wrapper, as both thin and thick work great with this method. But this recipe is adaptable to all sorts of dumpling shapes and cooking styles from guo-tie to shumai, so feel free to play around and find what suits your personal preferences best.

2 cups all-purpose flour, plus more for dusting

¾ cup warm water

Makes 24 wrappers

1 Place the flour in a medium mixing bowl. Gently pour in the water, incorporating it with the flour with a silicone spatula until loosely combined.

2 Transfer the dough to a lightly floured work surface and knead until smooth, about 10 minutes.

3 Wrap the dough in plastic wrap and let rest at room temperature for 30 minutes.

4 Dust the work surface with flour, then cut the dough into 4 pieces.

5 Roll each piece into a small log.

6 Cut each log into 6 approximately 1-inch pieces, then sprinkle with a generous amount of flour.

7 Place each piece on your work surface, cut side up. With the palm of your hand, press down to make a roughly flattened circle.

8 Dust both sides of the circle with flour. Using a rolling pin, roll around the edges to create a circular wrapper of your desired thinness.

9 Cover with plastic wrap so they don't dry out. If you're not folding dumplings right away, dust with flour or cornstarch on both sides of the wrappers. Lay the wrappers flat on a large tray or plate (their edges can slightly overlap to save space) and cover with plastic wrap. Store in the fridge for up to a day.

Until this book, I'd never made a gluten-free dumpling wrapper. However, the internet, my friends, and my agent have all begged me to develop one. So here it is—the closest I can get to a wrapper that doesn't sacrifice texture for dietary restrictions. It's not exactly the same as a classic wrapper, but it feels close! I optimized for a perfectly chewy QQ texture over foldability, so you'll find that this wrapper will not want to stretch as much as its gluten-full cousins. However, this dough, with some gentle handling, can accommodate all the folds shown in this book.

In a medium mixing bowl, combine the chickpea flour, tapioca flour, sweet rice flour, and xanthan gum. Slowly pour in the water, mixing with a silicone spatula to incorporate until all the water has been poured in and chunks have formed. Scoop out the clumps of dough and transfer to a lightly floured work surface. Knead until it forms a smooth ball. Follow steps in the Dumpling Wrappers recipe (page 120) to shape into dumpling wrappers, dusting with sweet rice flour instead of regular flour.

GLUTEN-FREE DUMPLING WRAPPERS

3 tablespoons plus 1 teaspoon chickpea flour

1 cup tapioca flour

1 cup sweet rice flour, plus more for dusting

1½ teaspoons xanthan gum

¾ cup plus 2 tablespoons water

Makes 24 wrappers

BAO OR GUA BAO WRAPPERS

This yeasted dough is made to be steamed to fluffy, moist perfection. It's delicious all on its own, with just salt and some scallions, but it truly shines as the base dough for classic steamed bao or gua bao.

1 tablespoon plus 1 teaspoon active dry yeast

2 teaspoons plus ¼ teaspoon granulated sugar

1½ cups warm water (95° to 115°F)

4 cups bread flour, plus more for dusting

½ teaspoon baking powder

¼ teaspoon baking soda

1 tablespoon kosher salt

Makes 24 wrappers

1 In a small mixing bowl, combine the yeast and the ¼ teaspoon sugar. Add the warm water and give it a little stir. Let it sit uncovered for 5 minutes to activate the yeast.

2 In a large mixing bowl, combine the bread flour, baking powder, baking soda, and salt. Pour in the activated yeast mixture.

3 Mix with a rubber spatula or wooden spoon until clumps form. Transfer to a lightly floured work surface and knead for 10 minutes until the dough is smooth like a baby's butt.

4 Place the dough in a large clean bowl and cover with plastic wrap. Proof at slightly warm room temperature (75°F is ideal) for 1 hour, until the dough doubles in size.

5 Transfer the dough back to the work surface and cut into 4 equal pieces.

6 Roll each piece into a large log.

7 Cut each log into 2 by 2-inch pieces approximately the size of marshmallows.

8 Place each piece on your work surface, cut side up. With the palm of your hand, press down to make a roughly flattened circle.

9a IF MAKING BAO WRAPPERS: Dust both sides of the circles with flour. Using a rolling pin, roll around the edges to create a circular wrapper of your desired thinness (or roll into an oval shape for gua bao). The wrapper is now ready to be filled and folded.

OR

9b IF MAKING GUA BAO WRAPPERS: Dust each side with flour and then, using a rolling pin, roll into an oval shape. Use an oiled chopstick to fold the oval in half to create a clamshell shape. Line a bamboo or metal steamer with a steamer liner or parchment paper with holes underneath, and place the gua bao wrappers on top, making sure to leave space between each one, as they'll expand. You may need multiple steamers if cooking all the wrappers. Place the steamer on top of a boiling pot of water and cover. Steam for 10 minutes, until cooked through.

COLORING DOUGH

Use these recipes as a 1:1 replacement for water in any dumpling or bao recipe. Coloring dough requires extracting pigment from pigment-rich ingredients. To color dough, blend an ingredient and strain it to get its concentrated juice, which is then added in place of the water in any dumpling or bao dough recipe. It has little to no effect on the flavor of the dough but provides a great natural food coloring. Some colors from ingredients stay vibrant throughout the entire cooking process, like the orange dough made from red bell peppers, while others, like purple cabbage dough might fade a little as it cooks, which is natural. The colors below are some of my favorites to work with, but I encourage you to experiment and find different ingredients and colors for your own doughs and noodles. Extra juice can be frozen in containers or ice cube trays to be reheated and used later.

 PURPLE COLORING

½ red cabbage, cored and coarsely chopped
1 cup water

In a powerful blender, combine the cabbage and water. Blend until completely smooth. Strain the mixture through a fine-mesh metal sieve, reserving the juice.

 MAGENTA COLORING

1 to 2 beets, peeled and chopped into rough chunks (use 1 beet for a lighter pink, and 2 for a magenta)
1 cup water

In a blender, combine the beets and water. Blend until smooth, then strain through a fine-mesh metal strainer, reserving the juice.

 RED COLORING

Combine 2 parts magenta coloring, 1 part orange to create red.

 MUSTARD COLORING

Combine 1 part orange coloring, 1 part green coloring to create mustard.

ORANGE COLORING

3 to 4 red bell peppers, stemmed, seeded, and coarsely chopped

In a blender, blend the peppers until smooth. (Red bell peppers hold quite a bit of water, but if they aren't blending smoothly, feel free to add water 1 tablespoon at a time.) Strain the mixture through a fine-mesh metal sieve, reserving the juice.

YELLOW COLORING

3 to 4 yellow bell peppers, stemmed, seeded, and coarsely chopped

In a blender, blend the peppers until smooth. (Bell peppers hold quite a bit of water, but if they aren't blending smoothly, feel free to add 1 tablespoon of water at a time.) Strain the mixture through a fine-mesh metal sieve, reserving the juice.

 PEACH COLORING

Combine 1 part orange coloring, 1 part purple coloring to create peach.

 BEIGE COLORING

Combine 1 part yellow coloring, 1 part purple coloring to create beige.

 GREEN COLORING

1 to 2 heaping handfuls of spinach (use 1 handful for a lighter green, and 2 for a darker green)
1 to 2 cups water

In a blender, combine the spinach and water. Blend until smooth, then strain through a fine-mesh metal sieve, reserving the juice.

 BLACK COLORING

Squid ink

Mix approximately 1 teaspoon of squid ink for every cup of water to create black. Use less squid ink to create grays and more squid ink to create true blacks

 WHITE COLORING

Just use water!

Dumpling & Bao Fillings

If one phrase could wholeheartedly sum up my life, it would be, "I love carbs." More specifically, I love things wrapped in carbs: dumplings, empanadas, gyros, momos, burritos, white bread . . . I could go on and on. I should probably just go and tell my therapist that "wrapped in carbs" is my first love language and to amend "quality time" to a distant second. But I'm getting off track here. Dumplings and bao, my first true wrapped-in-a-carb loves, would not be what they are without their fillings. Although seemingly simple, fillings are the flavor-packed heart of a dumpling or bao. When done right, they work in combination with their wrapper to create an amazingly flavorful, textural experience.

Fillings for Perfect Dumplings
A filling is a sum of many parts, an equation consisting of a primary flavor and texture plus secondary flavors and textures, followed by aromatics and seasoning. In my very subjective nonscientific opinion, a pork-and-cabbage dumpling is the perfect dumpling. Its primary flavor profile is juicy, meaty pork, complemented by a secondary flavor of napa cabbage that offers saltiness and crunch. The aromatics of garlic, ginger, and scallions round things out, adding freshness and complexity. It's the perfect formula for a well-balanced, highly successful dumpling that can be used as a base for other dumpling fillings as well.

Making Your Own Dumplings

1.
CHOOSE YOUR PRIMARY FILLING

(1 POUND TOTAL FOR 24 DUMPLINGS)

The primary filling is your protein, ideally a ground meat that has at least 20% fat content. If going vegetarian, use firm tofu or tofu skin.

GROUND PORK

The original, and still classic, filling for many dumplings and bao, it has a perfect proportion of protein to fat.

CHICKEN THIGH

A wonderful alternative to ground pork. I typically buy boneless, skinless thighs and grind them in a food processor.

SHRIMP

I personally love using shrimp as a complement to another protein. Instead of a full pound, I typically split the difference and do ½ pound shrimp and ½ pound pork or chicken. Try different proportions and see what works best for you.

2.
CHOOSE YOUR SECONDARY FILLING

(½ POUND TO 1 POUND)

A secondary filling typically is a vegetable or secondary protein that complements the primary filling in flavor or texture, or both.

FRESHNESS
- Bok choy
- Fennel
- Kale
- Napa cabbage
- Spinach
- Taiwanese cabbage

SWEET COMFORT
- Roasted bell peppers
- Roasted butternut squash
- Roasted carrots
- Roasted corn
- Roasted golden beets
- Roasted parsnips
- Roasted rutabaga
- Roasted sweet potato

SWEET-TART FLAVOR
- Apples
- Peaches
- Kimchi

MEATINESS
- Sautéed mushrooms
- Scrambled eggs
- Tofu
- Tofu skin

3.
CHOOSE YOUR AROMATICS

(ABOUT 1 CUP, MINCED)

Aromatics, like alliums, fresh herbs, and chiles, add a burst of flavor that enhances the primary and secondary fillings.

FRESH
- Chinese chives
- Garlic
- Ginger
- Ramps
- Scallions
- Shallots
- Basil
- Chives
- Cilantro
- Lemongrass
- Parsley
- Shiso

WOODSY
- Rosemary
- Sage
- Thyme
- Tarragon

4.
CHOOSE YOUR SEASONING

Highlight your filling ingredients with salt, sugar, oils, and/or ground spices.

SALTY
(up to 1 tablespoon)
- Kosher salt
- Miso
- Soy sauce

SWEET
(up to 1 tablespoon)
- Honey
- Maple syrup
- Mirin
- Sugar

NUTTY
- Toasted sesame oil

PUNCHY
- Garlic
- Ginger

TART
- Black vinegar
- Rice vinegar
- Lemon juice
- Sumac

SPICY
- Black or white pepper
- Chili crisp
- Red chilis

WARM
- Ground cinnamon
- Ground cumin
- Star anise

How to Fold Dumplings

Dumpling and bao folding can be as simple or complex as you want it to be. In the end, it's all about sealing the filling inside its dough companion. I've spent my entire childhood folding dumplings around a kitchen island with my family and even I still make dumplings that look like doughy turds almost every time I fold, and that's okay! As long as it's sealed, that dumpling will still taste just as delicious as that perfectly pleated one. These diagrams are step by step guides to some of my favorite folds—use them to follow along or as inspiration to make up your own unique folds.

Joining Colored Doughs

HOMESTYLE FOLD

SHUMAI FOLD / SHUMAI FOLD WITH CHIVE

Cooking Dumplings & Bao

There are three main ways of cooking a dumpling—boiling, pan-frying, and steaming. For each of the dumpling recipes that follow, I've recommended the cooking method I prefer for that recipe, but feel free to cook them any way you like. I love boiled dumplings when I make thicker wrappers, as the dough holds up well in a rolling boil and gives the finished dumpling a satisfying chew. Pan-fried dumplings are always a family favorite; the classic crispy bottom with a chewier top is texture bliss. Steamed dumplings are another classic preparation; I find this method lends itself best to delicate dumplings with thinner wrappers.

Boiling

Bring a large pot of water to a boil. Place dumplings into the pot with a slotted spoon. Let sit for a couple minutes, until the water is boiling again. Pour ½ cup of cold water into the pot to settle the boiling water back down (this will allow the filling to cook without having the wrappers break apart). When the water comes to a second boil and the dumplings float to the surface, they should be done. Cut into one to make sure the filling is cooked. If it needs more time, repeat the process with another ½ cup of cold water. Use a strainer to fetch the dumplings from the water, and serve.

Pan-Frying

In a large nonstick pan over medium-high heat, warm 1 tablespoon of neutral oil and place the dumplings in the pan, bottoms down. Fry for 1 to 2 minutes, until the bottoms have browned. Add ½ cup of water to the pan and place a lid on top (the water will splatter when it hits the oil, so be careful!). Reduce the heat to medium and steam for 6 to 8 minutes, adding more water, 1 tablespoon at a time, if the water evaporates. Fetch the dumplings from the pan, and serve.

Steaming

Line a bamboo or metal steamer with a steamer liner or parchment paper liner with precut holes. Place the dumplings in the steamer. Fill a pot that will fit your steamer with an inch of water and bring to a boil. Place the steamer in the pot and cover. Steam for 8 to 10 minutes, until cooked through, and serve.

CLASSIC PORK DUMPLINGS

This recipe has been a constant thread in our family, a communal ritual shared between three generations huddled around a kitchen island, all covered in flour while folding dumplings and talking nonsense together. A classic combination of pork and napa cabbage beloved by many families, it's a recipe that uses simple ingredients but provides maximum flavor through techniques I've learned watching my grandma since childhood. For example, she always grinds her own pork shoulder to provide the utmost freshness (although fresh, good-quality packaged ground pork works just fine if you don't have a meat grinder). She also salts diced napa cabbage and then squeezes it to release excess water, a technique that allows the cabbage to soak up pork juices later and prevents cabbage liquid from diluting the filling. She even taste-tests the filling by microwaving a small pea-size amount for 20 seconds (so it's fully cooked), and then adjusts seasonings as needed before folding. It's these little rituals of ingenuity that make a grandma's dumplings so special. Dumplings take time, especially the first go-around, but they're worth the effort—especially when done with friends, family, and good conversation.

DOUGH

1 recipe Dumpling Wrappers (page 120)

FILLING

½ medium head (1 pound) of napa cabbage

1 tablespoon plus ½ teaspoon kosher salt

1 pound ground pork or freshly ground pork shoulder

3 scallions, green and white parts, chopped

1 teaspoon minced fresh ginger

1 tablespoon minced fresh garlic (about 3 cloves)

2 teaspoons light brown sugar

2 teaspoons toasted sesame oil

1 tablespoon chicken stock

Makes about 24 dumplings

Tip:
A good rule of thumb for dumplings is to start making the filling while the wrapper dough is taking its 30-minute rest.

Photo:
These dumplings are made with the classic fold (page 131).

MAKE THE FILLING: In a large mixing bowl, combine the cabbage and the ½ teaspoon salt. Mix with your fingers to incorporate the salt throughout. Set the cabbage aside to sweat out water for about 10 minutes. Meanwhile, in another large mixing bowl, combine the ground pork, scallions, ginger, garlic, the remaining 1 tablespoon salt, brown sugar, sesame oil, and chicken stock.

After the cabbage has sweated out all its water, transfer it onto a thin dish towel or a few layers of thick paper towels and wrap around the cabbage to enclose. Using your hands and brute strength, squeeze out as much excess water from the cabbage as you can. Transfer the cabbage to the rest of the filling mixture and use your hands to mix all that juicy meat-mixture goodness together, using a circular motion, until the filling looks homogeneous and feels sticky, about 3 minutes. Cover the bowl with plastic wrap and set aside in the fridge until ready to form the dumplings, up to a day in advance.

FOLD THE DUMPLINGS: When ready to fold, place a spoonful of filling about a third the size of the wrapper into the center of the wrapper. Seal the dumpling using the fold of your choice (see pages 131–136). Repeat until you've run out of filling or wrappers. Tip: Stir-fry the extra filling and eat with rice for a delicious second meal.

BOIL THE DUMPLINGS: Bring a large pot of water to a boil. Place dumplings into the pot with a slotted spoon. Let sit for a couple minutes, until the water is boiling again. Pour ½ cup of cold water into the pot to settle the boiling water back down (this will allow the filling to cook without having the wrappers break apart). When the water comes to a second boil and the dumplings float to the surface, they should be done. Cut into one to make sure the filling is cooked. If it needs more time, repeat the process with another ½ cup of cold water. Use a strainer to fetch the dumplings from the water, and serve.

This vegetable dumpling aims for the gold standard set by Din Tai Fung, the famous Taiwanese dumpling restaurant chain I could eat at every day. Many vegetable dumpling recipes end up soggy, their chopped ingredients releasing water as they cook. To avoid this, the key is to prep the vegetables to maximize their individual flavors while minimizing excess moisture. Shiitake mushrooms are pan-sautéed and seasoned to bring out their umami flavor and meatiness, while bok choy is blanched to render it sweet and then squeezed of all its water to become a sponge for flavor. The preparation may seem tedious, but the resulting dumpling is as rich with textures and flavors as a meat-filled dumpling.

CLASSIC VEGETABLE GUO-TIE

PREP THE BOK CHOY: Bring a large pot of water to a boil. Add the bok choy and cook until it's cooked through and semi soft, 2 to 3 minutes. Carefully remove the bok choy (you can save this water for cooking the noodles later if you want) and rinse it under cold water to stop the cooking. Finely chop the bok choy and transfer it onto a thin dish towel or a few layers of thick paper towels and wrap around the bok choy to enclose. Using your hands and brute strength, squeeze out as much excess water from the bok choy as you can. Transfer to a bowl and set aside.

PREP THE RICE NOODLES: Bring a large fresh pot of water to a boil, or return the bok choy water to a boil. Cook the rice noodles according to package instructions, and drain. Rinse the noodles under cold water, and cut into ¼-inch pieces until you have ½ cup of chopped noodles. Set aside.

PREP THE TOFU: Dice the tofu skin into ¼-inch pieces until you have ½ cup chopped. Set aside.

PREP THE MUSHROOMS: In a small skillet over medium-high heat, warm a generous glug of canola oil. Add the garlic and stir for about 30 seconds, until the oil is seasoned with garlicky goodness. Add the mushrooms and stir until soft and cooked through, 3 to 4 minutes. Season with salt to taste. Transfer to a bowl and set aside.

MAKE THE FILLING: In a large mixing bowl, combine the bok choy, noodles, scallions, tofu skin, mushrooms, ½ teaspoon salt, brown sugar, sesame oil, and soy sauce and mix until incorporated. Cover the bowl with plastic wrap and place in the fridge until ready to form the dumplings, up to a day ahead.

FOLD THE DUMPLINGS: When ready to fold, place a spoonful of filling about a third the size of the wrapper into the center of the wrapper. Seal the dumpling using the fold of your choice (see pages 131–136). Repeat until you've run out of filling or wrappers. Tip: If you have extra vegetable filling, it tastes great stir-fried and served over a mound of white rice or tossed with fresh greens to make a salad.

PAN-FRY THE DUMPLINGS: In a large nonstick pan over medium-high heat, warm 1 tablespoon neutral oil and place the dumplings in the pan, bottoms down. Fry for 1 to 2 minutes, until the bottoms have browned. Add ½ cup of water to the pan and place a lid on top (the water will splatter when it hits the oil, so be careful!). Reduce the heat to medium and steam for 6 to 8 minutes, adding more water, 1 tablespoon at a time, if the water evaporates. Fetch the dumplings from the pan, and serve.

DOUGH
1 recipe Dumpling Wrappers (page 120)

FILLING
4 bok choy, bottoms trimmed

1½ ounces thin rice noodles

½ cup tofu skin (fried bean curd)

Canola oil, vegetable oil, or other neutral oil, plus more for pan frying

1 garlic clove, minced

½ pound shiitake mushrooms, stemmed and diced

4 scallions, green and white parts, chopped

½ teaspoon kosher salt, plus more as needed

1 teaspoon light brown sugar

1 teaspoon toasted sesame oil

1 tablespoon soy sauce

Makes about 24 dumplings

Photo:
These dumplings are made with green dough (page 126) and the classic fold (page 131).

CHICKEN, FENNEL, AND APPLE GUO-TIE

I love making dumplings based on the seasonal ingredients of wherever I happen to be in the moment. When I lived in San Francisco, a food lover's dream full of markets and co-ops filled with vibrant produce from local farms just across the bridge, I loved experimenting with anything I could find. Every market aisle was a playground for locating nontraditional flavor combinations. Back at home, I made dumplings using my grandma's techniques. This recipe was developed during a San Francisco autumn, when apples were in season. I love anything apple paired with meat, a combination used in some of my favorite foods, like Korean bulgogi and grilled chicken apple sausages. In this dumpling, sweet apple and savory chicken merge, and pickled fennel is the lightly acidic bridge that brings the two divergent flavor profiles together. I usually pan-fry these dumplings as a nod to all the roasted sausages I loved during college, but they are just as delicious steamed or boiled.

DOUGH

1 recipe Dumpling Wrappers (page 120)

FILLING

1 fennel bulb, trimmed and finely diced

1 tablespoon plus 1/4 teaspoon kosher salt

1 pound boneless, skinless chicken thighs

1 apple, peeled, cored, and grated

4 garlic cloves, finely grated

1/2 teaspoon grated fresh ginger

2 teaspoons light brown sugar

1 teaspoon toasted sesame oil

1/2 teaspoon soy sauce

Neutral oil for pan frying

Makes about 24 dumplings

Photo:
These dumplings are made with the classic round fold (page 135).

PREP THE FENNEL: In a medium mixing bowl, combine the fennel with the 1/4 teaspoon salt and mix with your hands until incorporated. Let the fennel sit for 5 to 10 minutes to sweat out water. Transfer the fennel to a thin dish cloth or some paper towels and squeeze out all the excess water. Set aside.

PREP THE CHICKEN: In a food processor, blend the chicken thighs until thoroughly ground.

MAKE THE FILLING: In a large mixing bowl, combine the fennel, chicken, apple, garlic, ginger, remaining 1 tablespoon salt, brown sugar, sesame oil, and soy sauce. With your hands, using a circular motion, mix together until the filling looks homogenous and feels sticky, about 3 minutes. Cover the bowl with plastic wrap and set aside in the fridge until ready to form the dumplings, up to a day in advance.

FOLD THE DUMPLINGS: When ready to fold, place a spoonful of filling about a third the size of the wrapper into the center of the wrapper. Seal the dumpling using the fold of your choice (see pages 131–136). Repeat until you've run out of filling or wrappers. Tip: If you have extra filling, stir-fry and eat with a bowl of rice or form into meatballs and roast on a parchment paper–lined sheet pan in a 400°F oven for 20 minutes until cooked through.

PAN-FRY THE DUMPLINGS: In a large nonstick pan over medium-high heat, warm 1 tablespoon neutral oil and place the dumplings in the pan, bottoms down. Fry for 1 to 2 minutes, until the bottoms have browned. Add 1/2 cup of water to the pan and place a lid on top (the water will splatter when it hits the oil, so be careful!). Reduce the heat to medium and steam for 6 to 8 minutes, adding more water, 1 tablespoon at a time, if the water evaporates. Fetch the dumplings from the pan, and serve.

Trader Joe's butternut squash ravioli singlehandedly carried me through college. Every decadent forkful of it made me feel like a five-star chef, even though my only job was to boil. This dumpling is an ode to that ravioli. Sweet roasted squash is pureed with the subtle spice of cinnamon and a hint of garlic and thyme. Its dense texture is complemented by fatty ground pork, while sesame oil and soy sauce bring it home to my roots. It's a perfect winter dumpling. I recommend pan-frying this one to get a nice crust on the wrapper; the crunch of the crust is the perfect contrast to the softer squash filling.

BUTTERNUT SQUASH AND PORK GUO-TIE

PREP THE BUTTERNUT SQUASH: Preheat the oven to 400°F. Line two baking sheets with parchment paper. With a knife or mandoline, cut the squash crosswise into paper-thin slices. Place the squash on the baking sheet in a single layer and drizzle with olive oil. Season with salt and pepper, and toss with your hands to coat. Roast the squash for 20 to 25 minutes, until softened and with slightly browned edges. Let cool.

In a small saucepan over medium heat, warm 1 tablespoon oil. Add the garlic, thyme, and pine nuts, and toast, stirring, until fragrant, about 2 minutes. Remove and discard the thyme sprigs.

Scrape the remaining contents of the pan into a food processor and add the roasted squash and the water. Process until the mixture has the consistency of cookie dough.

MAKE THE FILLING: In a large mixing bowl, combine the squash mixture, pork, scallions, cinnamon, brown sugar, soy sauce, sesame oil, 1½ tablespoons salt, and ½ teaspoon pepper. With your hands, using a circular motion, mix together until the filling looks homogenous and feels sticky, about 3 minutes. Cover the bowl with plastic wrap and set aside in the fridge until ready to form the dumplings, up to a day in advance.

FOLD THE DUMPLINGS: When ready to fold, place a spoonful of filling about a third the size of the wrapper into the center of the wrapper. Seal the dumpling using the fold of your choice (see pages 131–136). Repeat until you've run out of filling or wrappers. Tip: When I have extra filling, I love stir-frying it with the Spicy Soy and Scallion Sauce (page 11) and noodles and topping with fresh scallions for a spicy warm noodle bowl.

PAN-FRY THE DUMPLINGS: In a large nonstick pan over medium-high heat, warm 1 tablespoon neutral oil and place the dumplings in the pan, bottoms down. Fry for 1 to 2 minutes, until the bottoms have browned. Add ½ cup of water to the pan and place a lid on top (the water will splatter when it hits the oil, so be careful!). Reduce the heat to medium and steam for 6 to 8 minutes, adding more water, 1 tablespoon at a time, if the water evaporates. Fetch the dumplings from the pan, and serve.

DOUGH

1 recipe Dumpling Wrappers (page 120)

FILLING

2 medium butternut squash, peeled, halved lengthwise, and seeds removed

Olive oil

Kosher salt and freshly ground black pepper

1 whole garlic clove

2 sprigs thyme

1 tablespoon pine nuts

1 tablespoon water

¾ pound ground pork

3 scallions, green and white parts, chopped

⅛ teaspoon, ground cinnamon

1 teaspoon light brown sugar

1 teaspoon soy sauce

1 teaspoon toasted sesame oil

Neutral oil for pan frying

Makes about 24 dumplings

Photo, middle:
These dumplings are made with orange dough (page 126) and the braided fold (page 136).

CHILI CRISP CHICKEN AND PEACH GUO-TIE

Here's a bright, subtly spicy summertime pan-fried dumpling for when peaches are in season. I've never seen my family put peaches into dumplings, but in my whirlwind of experimentation with seasonal produce I've always been delightfully surprised by how well the sweetness of ripe peaches lends itself to the flavors of a traditional dumpling filling. Where peaches lend sweetness, the remaining filling is balanced out with the Avengers of flavor, including fattiness from ground chicken thigh, spiciness from chili crisp, and a hit of acid from ketchup and rice vinegar.

DOUGH

1 recipe Dumping Wrappers (page 120)

Neutral oil for pan frying

FILLING

4 medium carrots, trimmed and halved lengthwise

Olive oil

1 pound boneless, skinless chicken thighs, ground

½ ripe peach, peeled, pitted, and finely grated

3 garlic cloves, finely grated

1 teaspoon finely grated fresh ginger

1 teaspoon rice vinegar

1 tablespoon chili crisp

1 tablespoon ketchup

2 teaspoons toasted sesame oil

2 teaspoons light brown sugar

1 tablespoon kosher salt, plus more as needed

Makes about 24 dumplings

Photo:
These dumplings are made with orange dough (page 126) and the classic fold (page 135).

MAKE THE FILLING: Preheat the oven to 400°F. Line a baking sheet with parchment paper. Place the carrots on the prepared sheet and drizzle with olive oil. Toss with your hands to coat, and season with salt to taste. Roast for 25 minutes, until the carrots are soft and can be pierced easily with a fork. Transfer the carrots to a work surface and finely dice. Transfer to a large mixing bowl and add the chicken, peach, garlic, ginger, rice vinegar, chili crisp, ketchup, sesame oil, brown sugar, and 1 tablespoon salt. With your hands, using a circular motion, mix together until the filling looks homogenous and feels sticky, about 3 minutes. Cover the bowl with plastic wrap and set aside in the fridge until ready to form the dumplings, up to a day in advance.

FOLD THE DUMPLINGS: When ready to fold, place a spoonful of filling about a third the size of the wrapper into the center of the wrapper. Seal the dumpling using the fold of your choice (see pages 131–136). Repeat until you've run out of filling or wrappers.

PAN-FRY THE DUMPLINGS: In a large nonstick pan over medium-high heat, warm 1 tablespoon neutral oil and place the dumplings in the pan, bottoms down. Fry for 1 to 2 minutes, until the bottoms have browned. Add ½ cup of water to the pan and place a lid on top (the water will splatter when it hits the oil, so be careful!). Reduce the heat to medium and steam for 6 to 8 minutes, adding more water, 1 tablespoon at a time, if it evaporates. Fetch the dumplings from the pan, and serve.

Tip:
If you have extra filling, this makes a great topping for a noodle bowl. Just stir-fry alongside your cooked noodles, then toss with Spicy Soy Scallion Sauce (page 11) and serve, topped with chopped scallions and extra chili crisp.

In this vegetable-forward shumai, golden beets are the star. Caramelized in the oven, they provide the perfect earthy companion. Their slightly sweet nature and robust texture pair well with the traditional dumpling filling of ground pork. Here, the pork plays a supporting role, adding just a bit of satisfying fat into the mix for balance. To make this shumai vegetarian/vegan, you can easily substitute firm tofu for the pork.

ROASTED GOLDEN BEETS AND PORK SHUMAI

PREP THE BEETS: Preheat the oven to 400°F. Line a baking sheet with parchment paper. With a knife or mandoline (careful with those fingertips!), cut the beets into thin slices (the size of a thick potato chip). Arrange the slices evenly on the prepared baking sheet and drizzle with olive oil to coat. Roast for 12 to 15 minutes, until soft. Remove from the oven, and once they are cool enough to handle, dice them and set aside.

PREP THE CABBAGE: In a large mixing bowl, combine the cabbage and the ½ teaspoon salt. Mix with your fingers to incorporate the salt throughout. Set the cabbage aside to sweat out water for about 10 minutes. Transfer to a thin dish towel or a few layers of thick paper towels and wrap around the cabbage to enclose. Using your hands and brute strength, squeeze out as much excess water from the cabbage as you can.

MAKE THE FILLING: In a large mixing bowl, combine the cabbage, diced beets, pork, scallions, garlic, ginger, brown sugar, and the remaining 1 tablespoon salt. With your hands, using a circular motion, mix together until the filling looks homogenous and feels sticky, about 3 minutes. Cover the bowl with plastic wrap and set aside in the fridge until ready to form the dumplings, up to a day in advance.

FOLD THE DUMPLINGS: When ready to fold, place a spoonful of filling about a third the size of the wrapper into the center of the wrapper. Seal the dumpling using the shumai fold (see page 134). Repeat until you've run out of filling or wrappers. Tip: The mixture of golden beets and pork makes a great salty-sweet addition when scrambled with eggs for a hearty breakfast.

STEAM THE SHUMAI: Line a bamboo or metal steamer with a steamer liner or parchment paper liner with precut holes. Place the dumplings in the steamer. Fill a pot that will fit your steamer with an inch of water and bring to a boil. Place the steamer in the pot and cover. Steam for 8 to 10 minutes, until the meat has cooked through, and serve.

DOUGH

1 recipe Dumpling Wrappers (page 120)

FILLING

3 small-to-medium golden beets, peeled

Olive oil

½ napa cabbage, minced

1 tablespoon plus ½ teaspoon kosher salt

½ pound ground pork

3 scallions, green and white parts, chopped

3 garlic cloves, finely grated

1 teaspoon finely grated fresh ginger

1½ teaspoons light brown sugar

Makes about 24 dumplings

Photo:
These dumplings are made with green dough (page 126) and the shumai fold with chive (page 134).

PORK BELLY MUSHROOM SHUMAI IN CORN SOUP

Carbs, like humans, love soaking in a big bath of hot liquid—think an umami bowl of tonkatsu ramen, the comfort of matzo ball soup, a soothing spoonful of congee. A floating package of delight in its natural element, bobbing along in a sea of warm broth, a dumpling is no exception. This recipe plays off this natural combination, pairing creamy corn soup with meaty pork and mushroom shumai. Each dumpling is packed with pork belly, shiitake mushrooms, and Taiwanese cabbage (a variety found in Asian supermarkets and known for its sweetness). Creamy soups aren't traditionally used as a base for dumplings, but naturally I wanted to combine memories of eating my dad's corn soup and my grandma's pork dumplings into one evocative bite.

DOUGH

1 recipe Dumpling Wrappers (page 120)

FILLING

5 cups finely diced Taiwanese cabbage or napa cabbage (from ½ large head)

½ pound pork belly, skin removed, ground or very finely chopped

½ pound ground pork

1 cup chopped shiitake mushrooms

1 tablespoon minced garlic (3 cloves)

2 teaspoons finely grated fresh ginger

1 tablespoon plus ½ teaspoon kosher salt

4 teaspoons light brown sugar

1 teaspoon toasted sesame oil

BROTH

1 recipe Creamy Corn Soup (page 35)

TOPPINGS (OPTIONAL)

Chopped scallions

Scallion Oil (page 11)

Makes about 24 dumplings

Photo:
These dumplings are made with the shumai fold (page 134).

PREP THE CABBAGE: In a large mixing bowl, combine the cabbage and the ½ teaspoon salt. Mix with your fingers to incorporate the salt throughout. Set the cabbage aside to sweat out water for about 10 minutes. Meanwhile, in a large mixing bowl, combine the pork belly, ground pork, mushrooms, garlic, ginger, remaining 1 tablespoon salt, brown sugar, and sesame oil.

MAKE THE FILLING: After the cabbage has sweated out all its water, transfer it onto a thin dish towel or a few layers of thick paper towels and wrap around the cabbage to enclose. Using your hands and brute strength, squeeze out as much excess water from the cabbage as you can. Transfer the cabbage to the rest of the filling mixture and with your hands, using a circular motion, mix together until the filling looks homogenous and feels sticky, about 3 minutes. Cover the bowl with plastic wrap and set aside in the fridge until ready to form the dumplings, up to a day in advance.

FOLD THE DUMPLINGS: When ready to fold, place a spoonful of filling about a third the size of the wrapper into the center of the wrapper. Seal the dumpling using the shumai fold (see page 134). Repeat until you've run out of filling or wrappers. Tip: If you have extra filling, I like to form into meatballs and boil directly in Chicken Stock (page 12) for 10 to 15 minutes, until the meatballs are firm and cooked through, then adding some extra napa cabbage leaves or pea shoots.

PREP THE BROTH: In a pot over low heat, warm the creamy corn soup. Keep at a low simmer until ready to serve.

STEAM THE SHUMAI: Line a bamboo or metal steamer with a steamer liner or parchment paper liner with precut holes. Place the dumplings in the steamer. Fill a pot that will fit your steamer with an inch of water and bring to a boil. Place the steamer in the pot and cover. Steam for 8 to 10 minutes, until the meat has cooked through. Divide the soup among 4 shallow bowls and place 6 shumai in the middle of each bowl. If using, garnish with scallions and a drizzle of scallion oil, and serve.

I love using my grandma's dumpling techniques with ingredients that she might've not necessarily chosen. This recipe marries classic ground pork with aromatic fresh basil and maple syrup. Onions provide additional natural sweetness and subtle texture in place of the traditional napa cabbage (but I do use my grandma's technique of salting and squeezing to drain the onion's excess water so it can become a sponge for flavor). Scallions, garlic, and ginger round out the rest of the flavors to create a filling full of contrasting tastes and textures. Pork is usually my go-to for the meat in this dumpling, but freshly ground chicken thigh makes a great substitute.

MAPLE PORK AND BASIL DUMPLINGS

PREP THE ONIONS: In a large mixing bowl, combine the onions and the ½ teaspoon salt. Mix with your fingers to incorporate the salt throughout. Set the onions aside to sweat out water for about 10 minutes. Transfer to a thin dish towel or a few layers of thick paper towels and wrap around the onions to enclose. Using your hands and brute strength, squeeze out as much excess water from the onions as you can.

MAKE THE FILLING: In a large mixing bowl, combine the onions, pork, ginger, garlic, scallions, basil, maple syrup, and the remaining 1 tablespoon salt. With your hands, using a circular motion, mix together until the filling looks homogeneous and feels sticky, about 3 minutes. Cover the bowl with plastic wrap and set aside in the fridge until ready to form the dumplings, up to a day in advance.

FOLD THE DUMPLINGS: When ready to fold, place a spoonful of filling about a third the size of the wrapper into the center of the wrapper. Seal the dumpling using the fold of your choice (see pages 131–136). Repeat until you've run out of filling or wrappers. Tip: If you have extra filling and have a pizza night, crumble some of this mixture onto your pizza. It pairs seamlessly with tomato sauce, fresh mozzarella, and olives.

PAN-FRY THE DUMPLINGS: In a large nonstick pan over medium-high heat, warm 1 tablespoon neutral oil and place the dumplings in the pan, bottoms down. Fry for 1 to 2 minutes, until the bottoms have browned. Add ½ cup of water to the pan and place a lid on top (the water will splatter when it hits the oil, so be careful!). Reduce the heat to medium and steam for 6 to 8 minutes, adding more water, 1 tablespoon at a time, if the water evaporates. Fetch the dumplings from the pan, and serve garnished with chives, basil, and a drizzle of scallion oil.

DOUGH

1 recipe Dumpling Wrappers (page 120)

FILLING

1 small sweet onion, finely diced

1 tablespoon plus ½ teaspoon kosher salt

1 pound ground pork

1 teaspoon grated fresh ginger

4 garlic cloves, grated

2 scallions, green and white parts, chopped

¼ cup plus 2 tablespoons minced basil (1 large bunch)

1 tablespoon plus 1 teaspoon maple syrup

Neutral oil for pan frying

GARNISH

Chopped chives

Chopped basil

Scallion Oil (page 11)

Makes about 24 dumplings

Photo:
These dumplings are made with the classic round fold (page 135).

ROASTED CARROT AND PORK BAO

These steamy, juicy pork and roasted carrot bao take me back to a specific place: my grandma's small Memphis kitchen, somewhere I barely visited growing up and the reason why I have such a strong yearning to embrace my Taiwanese identity. Passed down from my grandma, these steamed bao fed me on every Thanksgiving visit to Memphis until I was plump with joy. This dish takes time, technique, and a little upper-body strength, but it's so worth the effort. The carrots are caramelized in the oven before being mixed into the filling, a trick that adds complexity. Ground pork is the classic meat filling of choice, but feel free to swap it with other meats with some fat, like ground chicken thigh, or to replace half the pork with shrimp.

DOUGH

1 recipe Bao
Wrappers
(page 124)

FILLING

12 medium carrots,
ends trimmed

4 tablespoons
olive oil

5 teaspoons
kosher salt

2 pounds
ground pork

8 scallions, green
and white parts,
chopped

6 garlic cloves,
minced

2 teaspoons minced
fresh ginger

2 teaspoons
granulated sugar

2 teaspoons toasted
sesame oil

Makes 24 bao

Photo:
These dumplings are made with the
braided fold (page 136).

PREP THE CARROTS: Preheat the oven to 400°F. Line a baking sheet with parchment paper. Place the carrots on the prepared sheet and drizzle with the olive oil. Toss with your hands to coat, and season with salt to taste. Roast for 25 minutes, until the carrots are soft and can be pierced easily with a fork. Transfer the carrots to a large mixing bowl, and use a fork to mash them into small even chunks. Add the pork, scallions, garlic, ginger, 2 teaspoons salt, sugar, and sesame oil. With your hands, using a circular motion, mix together until the filling looks homogeneous and feels sticky, about 3 minutes. Cover the bowl with plastic wrap and set aside in the fridge until ready to form the dumplings, up to a day in advance.

FOLD THE BAO: When ready to fold, place a spoonful of filling about a third the size of the wrapper into the center of the wrapper. Seal the bao using the fold of your choice (see pages 131–136). Repeat until you've run out of filling or wrappers. Tip: If you have extra bao dough, form the remainder into balls (or go crazy and make wild shapes) and steam for a simple version of mantou, a basic steamed bun.

STEAM THE BAO: Line a bamboo or metal steamer with a steamer liner or parchment paper liner with precut holes. Place the bao in the steamer. Fill a pot that will fit your steamer with an inch of water and bring to a boil. Place the steamer in the pot and cover. Steam for 15 minutes, until cooked through. To test for doneness, cut into a bao to make sure the meat is fully cooked.

I love finding commonalities between my Taiwanese and American roots. Paying homage to the universal love language that marries an egg with a carb, this recipe is a mash-up of an Egg McMuffin and my aunt's flash-fried egg omelet.

Only half the Bao Wrappers recipe is used here. The steamed bao dough is shaped into sandwich buns and toasted in a pan for that perfect juxtaposition of fluffy and crisp bread, a method I've also come to know from eating many an In-N-Out burger. The bao is filled with a soft egg omelet as well as arugula, cheese, and a sweet-soy-glazed, thick-cut piece of bacon that brings me back to San Francisco's iconic millionaire's bacon. A spread of chili-crisp ketchup links my suburban refrigerator with my grandma's pantry for a kick of acid and spice to round out this Taiwanese American(ish) breakfast sandwich.

SHAPE THE BAO: Cut the dough into 6 even pieces and shape into balls. Proof for 1 hour in a warm, draft-free place until doubled in size.

STEAM THE BAO: Line a bamboo or metal steamer with a steamer liner or parchment paper liner with precut holes. Place the bao balls in the steamer, making sure to leave space between each one, as they'll expand (you may need multiple steamers or to steam in batches). Fill a pot that will fit your steamer with an inch of water and bring to a boil. Place the steamer in the pot and cover. Steam for 8 to 10 minutes, until cooked. Cut each bun into halves and set aside.

MAKE THE BACON: Preheat the oven to 350°F. Set a wire rack inside a rimmed baking sheet and spread out the bacon evenly on top. In a small mixing bowl, whisk together the soy sauce, honey, and red pepper flakes until smooth. Pour three-fourths of the glaze over the bacon, reserving one-fourth for glazing after it's cooked. Cook for 20 to 25 minutes, until slightly crisped. Cut the bacon into halves, drizzle with the remaining glaze, and set aside.

MAKE THE OMELETS: While the bacon cooks, start on the eggs: In a large mixing bowl, whisk together eggs, soy sauce, and honey. In a medium nonstick saucepan over medium-high heat, warm 2 tablespoons oil. Add a generous pinch of the scallions and stir for 30 seconds to 1 minute, until fragrant and sizzling. Add 1/4 cup of beaten egg mixture. As the eggs hit the pan, they will bubble and start to fry. Quickly stir with a spatula to scramble the eggs while they're in liquid form. As they start to solidify, stop scrambling and form them into a circular omelet roughly the size of the bao. Turn the heat down to medium and continue to cook, flipping once, until the omelet is cooked through. Repeat for the remaining eggs until you've made 6 omelets.

ASSEMBLE THE SANDWICHES: In a large saucepan over medium-high heat with a light drizzle of oil, toast the bao halves on both sides until lightly browned and crisp. Top a bao half with an omelet, a slice of cheese, a handful of arugula, and 2 pieces of bacon. Spread chili oil ketchup on another bao half and invert onto the sandwich, ketchup side down. Serve immediately.

BAO EGG AND SOY-GLAZED BACON SANDWICHES

BUNS

1/2 recipe Bao Wrappers (page 124)

BACON

1/2 pound thick-cut bacon, about 6 slices

2 tablespoons soy sauce

1/4 cup honey

1/4 teaspoon red pepper flakes

OMELETS

12 eggs, beaten

6 teaspoons soy sauce

3 teaspoons honey

Canola oil or vegetable oil

6 scallions, green and white parts, chopped

TOPPINGS

Sliced cheddar cheese

Arugula

Chili Oil Ketchup (page 12)

Makes 6 sandwiches

FRIED CHICKEN GUA BAO

This is the Taiwanese American version of a fried chicken sandwich. If I could be buried in a bucket of fried chicken, I would—I honestly love fried food that much. It's a consequence of growing up surrounded by Catholic school festivals bursting with greasy funnel cakes and corn dogs. Or maybe it was those weekly drive-through stops for Chicken McNuggets and extra-large french fries. Either way, I knew I had to pair Taiwanese fried chicken with steamed bao dough. Here, a fluffy and subtly sweet gua bao dough is the vehicle for the crunchiest Taiwanese fried chicken. Almond soy glaze adds a nutty balance to the saltiness of the chicken, while simple pickled cucumbers bring fresh acidity.

FILLING

2 pounds boneless, skinless chicken thighs

3 garlic cloves, minced

1 tablespoon soy sauce

2 tablespoons Shaoxing wine, mirin, or sake

1 teaspoon kosher salt

2 tablespoons all-purpose flour

1 egg white

One 14-ounce bag sweet potato starch

2 to 3 cups canola oil, vegetable oil, or any other oil with a high smoke point

Freshly ground black pepper

Makes 24 bao

DOUGH

1 recipe Gua Bao Wrappers (page 124)

All-purpose flour for dusting

Neutral oil for folding

TOPPINGS

Cold Marinated Pickles (page 22)

Thinly sliced scallions

Chopped cilantro

Almond Soy Glaze (page 11)

Chopped peanuts, almonds, or pine nuts

MAKE THE FILLING: Cut the chicken thighs into halves (for smaller pieces) and thirds (for larger pieces) so you have roughly even chunks. In a large mixing bowl, stir together the garlic, soy sauce, cooking wine, salt, flour, and egg white. Add the chicken pieces, cover the bowl, and marinate in the fridge for at least 1 hour and up to overnight.

STEAM THE BAO: Roll each wrapper into an oval shape. Oil a chopstick and place it in the center of the oval, folding the dough over it to create a clamshell shape. Line a bamboo or metal steamer with a steamer liner or parchment paper liner with precut holes. Place the gua bao wrappers in the steamer, making sure to leave space between each one, as they'll expand (you may need multiple steamers or to steam in batches). Fill a pot that will fit your steamer with an inch of water and bring to a boil. Place the steamer in the pot and cover. Steam for 15 minutes, until cooked through.

BATTER THE CHICKEN: Pour the sweet potato starch into a large mixing bowl. Remove the chicken from the marinade. Dip a chicken piece into the starch, turning to coat, and set aside on a plate. Repeat for all the chicken pieces.

FRY THE CHICKEN: Fill a large Dutch oven or heavy pot with 2 to 3 cups of oil (to reach a depth of about 3 inches). Set over high heat and warm until the oil temperature reaches 350° to 375°F. Line a tray with paper towels.

Fry the chicken in batches, turning as necessary, until lightly golden brown, 2 to 3 minutes per batch. Remove the chicken pieces with a mesh strainer and transfer to the prepared tray. When all the chicken has had its first fry, turn the heat up to high to get the oil to 385° to 395°F. For the final fry, place the chicken pieces back in the pot and flash-fry for 30 seconds to 1 minute, until golden brown. Transfer the chicken back to paper towels to drain. In a large mixing bowl, toss the chicken with a sprinkle of salt and pepper.

ASSEMBLE THE GUA BAO: Unfold a wrapper and fill with 1 to 2 pieces of fried chicken, a few pickles, scallions, and a shower of cilantro. Spoon the almond soy glaze over the chicken and top with some chopped nuts. Finally, pat yourself on the back for doing all that work, and savor the sweet-and-salty gua bao with a big bite.

This gua bao pays homage to the Asian American immigrant table. It's filled with a hodgepodge of flavors from various cultures—dishes together on a table that never resembled friends' dinner tables growing up but is steeped in tradition all the same. I grew up going to my grandma's house in Memphis where the table was filled with Corky's barbecue and steamed buns. I happily looked forward to these dishes every year when visiting my grandma for Thanksgiving, and her table was as American as one with a whole roasted turkey on it. This yearly pilgrimage to my grandma's Taiwanese kitchen in Memphis was where my love of barbecue grew. This recipe showcases slow roasted beef brisket that's slathered in a barbecue sauce made of black vinegar. A gua bao wrapper becomes the perfect vehicle for this succulent meat that's sliced and paired with pickles, scallions, and cilantro.

BLACK VINEGAR BARBECUE BEEF BRISKET GUA BAO

PREP THE BRISKET: The night before, in a small bowl, mix together all the ingredients for the dry rub. Pat the beef brisket dry and cover the entire surface with the rub. Place the meat on a rack that's sitting on a tray and refrigerate overnight.

COOK THE BRISKET: The next day, preheat the oven to 250°F. Place the meat the on a large piece of aluminum foil and tightly wrap around the meat to cover. Roast for 2½ hours.

MAKE THE BARBECUE SAUCE: While the meat is roasting, place the butter, ginger, and garlic in a medium saucepan over medium heat and cook until sizzling and fragrant. Add the onion and continue to cook, stirring occasionally, until the onion is semitransparent, about 5 minutes. Add the rest of the sauce ingredients and continue to stir together until incorporated. Once it's really bubbling, turn it down to a simmer and continue to cook for 5 minutes to thicken.

Place the sauce into a blender and blend until smooth. Store in the fridge until the meat is ready.

STEAM THE BAO: Roll each wrapper into an oval shape. Oil a chopstick and place it in the center of the oval, folding the dough over it to create a clamshell shape. Line a bamboo or metal steamer with a steamer liner or parchment paper liner with precut holes. Place the gua bao wrappers in the steamer, making sure to leave space between each one, as they'll expand (you may need multiple steamers or to steam in batches). Fill a pot that will fit your steamer with an inch of water and bring to a boil. Place the steamer in the pot and cover. Steam for 15 minutes, until cooked through.

FINISH ROASTING BRISKET: After 2½ hours, uncover the meat and brush with half the barbecue sauce (reserving the other half to serve). Turn the oven up to 350°F and roast the brisket uncovered for 30 minutes.

ASSEMBLE THE GUA BAO: Unfold a wrapper and fill with a few slices of brisket, a row of pickles, scallions, and a shower of cilantro. Spoon some extra barbecue sauce over the brisket, top with chopped nuts, and serve.

DOUGH

1 recipe Bao Wrappers (page 124)

DRY RUB

2 tablespoons light brown sugar

2 tablespoons kosher salt

1 teaspoon black pepper

1 teaspoon garlic powder

¼ teaspoon cumin

½ teaspoon orange zest

¼ teaspoon cinnamon

MEAT

3 pounds beef brisket

BARBECUE SAUCE

1 tablespoon butter

1 teaspoon grated fresh ginger

3 cloves garlic, sliced

½ sweet onion, diced

½ cup dark brown sugar

¼ cup soy sauce

2 tablespoons black vinegar

2 tablespoons ketchup

1 teaspoon mustard

½ teaspoon kosher salt

TOPPINGS

Cold Marinated Pickles (page 22)

Thinly sliced scallions

Chopped cilantro

Chopped peanuts, almonds, or pine nuts

Makes 24 bao

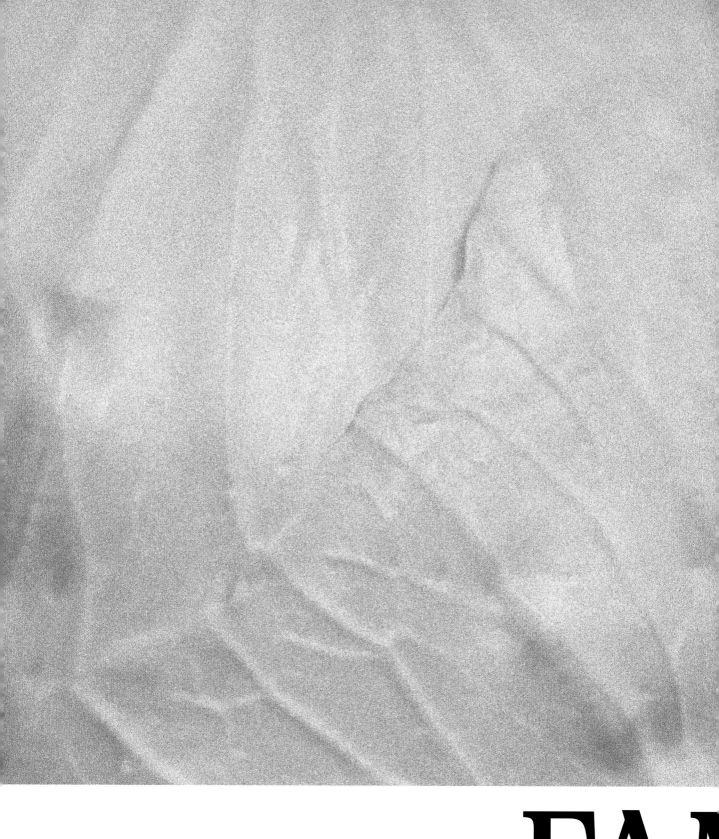

FAM

06

MILY STYLE

Dinners with Antoni Porowski

1

God, in the form of a shirtless Antoni Porowski from *Queer Eye,* asks me, "When are you most happy?" It's my thirtieth birthday, but I'm not at home in Seattle anymore. I'm sitting at a simple wooden table draped in crisp white linen, a valley of white clouds surrounding us. I look back at Antoni in a daze. I've always believed in a God. A faith that's been a part of me since childhood, wavering on and off as I've grown older, like a child playing with a light switch. My mind starts to wander. If God is Antoni, then Jonathan Van Ness must be . . . Jesus? A throat clears, catching my attention, as if Antoni knows exactly when my mind is trailing too far from reality. He politely asks again, "When are you most happy?"

Flashes of holidays and an abundance of food come to mind as I begin to pinpoint the answer to Antoni's question: during dinners with my family. I pause to notice that the table has been prepared, and I wonder who else might be coming. Just as Antoni catches my eye, he gives me a wink, and the entire floor drops.

I'm falling through the sky, but I don't feel any wind. Clouds rush past me until they twist away like wisps of steam as I'm enveloped in darkness. I search my surroundings for any signs of familiarity as a room begins to form around me. I feel a familiar lingering warmth and turn around to see my grandma delicately placing a whole fish in a bamboo steamer. I must be at my aunt's house in Denver, and dinner's almost ready.

I'm standing in a kitchen now as it comes alive with the crackle of scallions and ginger in a skillet and the voices of the women of my family. I watch as my aunt casually juliennes scallions into thin even slices with a precision I've only ever seen on *Top Chef*. My grandma insists I eat scallion buns she's just reheated while she simultaneously cleans her cookware to stir-fry the next dishes. I gladly accept a scallion bun, relishing the delight in always being full before I even sit at the table. The kitchen is bustling with a cacophony of ingredient prep and Mandarin as I watch two generations of women assemble our family's dishes.

I'm at the table as my plate gets filled to the brim. As the youngest in the family, I've grown up witnessing a special kind of magic trick—a plate that seems to always deliver the best cut of meat or the largest portion of vegetables. A plate that's somehow never empty no matter how much I eat. The wooden table is covered with a sea of dishes. Roasted pea shoots swimming in a garlicky broth. A Pyrex dish overflowing with halves of soy-marinated egg, slices of firm tofu, and juicy beef tendon. A whole steamed tilapia, cooked from head to tail, is revealed as my grandma lifts the lid of a bamboo steamer. A celebratory click of my iPhone camera captures it, to join other images from years past. My grandma places a generous fillet of steamed fish onto my plate. I quickly shovel it into my mouth, a tunnel vision of tender bliss overtaking my lack of hunger.

As I'm mid-bite, I notice Antoni sitting at the table. He looks back at me, giving me a little wave. Curious, I pause, knowing Antoni Porowski doesn't fit into this familiar setting. I look to my aunt, who is unfazed by his presence. She's too busy laboriously picking out all the bones in her scraps of steamed fish, gathering each tender flake for one perfect bite. My grandma, who would gladly comment on a chiseled specimen of a man, also carries on unbothered as she finally reaches for the steamed fish. Her chopsticks aim straight for the head, its foggy eyes staring back at me as it makes its annual descent to my grandma's plate. She picks at the fish head, noticing my disgust as she delightfully plucks out an eyeball and eats it with a smile. I motion toward the bounty of tender fish on my plate and gently slide it next to her fish head. But as the fish reaches her plate, it suddenly disappears, only to emerge back onto mine. I try to slide a fillet toward her again, which disappears and then reappears on my plate. I feel a sense of panic, staring at my overflowing plate of tender fish reemerging with every attempt. Why can't I just give my grandma what I have? My anxiety begins pulling me toward the floor as I grasp for reality. I search for my mom, only to find Antoni catch my eye once again. He gives me a wink, and I know what happens next.

2

I feel humidity first, a familiar heat that makes my skin feel like one large Post-it Note. It can only be Taipei in the summer. I'm in a cramped room with the blinds drawn, muffling the sounds of children playing in the street. I hear my mom's voice and instantly feel comfort in the constant stream of Mandarin that comes from a mother born to talk too much. As I approach her, my relief turns to surprise. Her typically well-kept, medium-length hair in various shades of dyed bronze is now cut into a short jet-black bob. Her signature dimples, a secret weapon typically on full display to get what she wants from men, are hidden now behind plumper cheeks. She's a teenager.

My mom is sitting at a wooden table along with her two sisters, my aunts, a youthfulness nearly disguising their identities. A young woman nearly my age is standing near a metal sink. She's thinly slicing scallions, the knife and her fingers in perpetual motion as she turns her head and beckons me to the table. She approaches me as I sit in the chair next to my mom. She places in front of me a large paperback workbook, a small No. 2 pencil, and a long rope. I stare, confused, pondering the significance of these objects. As my mind catches the faint wisp of steam from the stove, I suddenly feel the rope wrap around me, gently tightening its grip on my waist and legs. I turn, flustered, to face the woman with the rope draped in her hands, only to find the soft eyes of my grandma looking back at me. Her youthful eyes smiling with the same giving warmth as when she offers me scallion buns. I relent, and my grandma carefully wraps the rope around me, securing me to the chair.

I turn to my mom and aunts, noticing they too are each tied with a long rope, bound to the chair in an immovable grip around their waist and legs while their arms and hands freely turn the pages of the same large workbook I have in front of me. My gaze falls on the cover: *Vocabulary and Grammar for Children: An Introduction to English and the World of Opportunity.*

A trail of steam descends to the table, as my grandma lifts a lid to reveal a whole fish. My mom barely notices, continuing to scribble in her workbook, flipping page after page. The fish remains untouched, its plume of steam rising toward the ceiling and becoming a light thread. I watch my mom as a determined focus drives her to be the first to finish her workbook. I recognize her drive; it reminds me of what she passed on to me, a perpetual need to be so persistent that opportunity doesn't have a choice but to acknowledge you. "Cockroaches never die," she always says.

I watch as she finishes a final scribble. She closes her book and acknowledges the steamed fish for the first time. I suddenly see Antoni emerge. He gives me a quick nod as he approaches my mom, placing an empty plate down along with another workbook. He helps her untie the knots binding her as she stands with exasperation to reach for a spoonful of fish, savoring a single bite. As she finishes the bite, my mom begins retying the ropes, securing herself with a final knot back to the chair.

I feel sadness well up inside of me. I'm only just now seeing my lack of recognition of her past circumstances. Every car ride sitting shotgun, my mom driving, and all I remember is silence, with only the sounds of KISS 107-FM and the clicks of a Gameboy playing stupid Pokémon Pinball between us. Why did I never ask about her story? I think back to when I was thirteen. Every program she signed me up for that I begrudgingly attended, wanting to quit before even starting. Softball, club soccer, endurance swimming, piano and drawing lessons, Chinese school, Boy Scouts, gymnastics, tennis, Kumon, Catholic school—a world of opportunity for me.

She opens the next workbook, the next bite of fish awaiting her at the end. I turn to Antoni in pain, not from the ropes but instead from the tightening grip of guilt. He gives me a wink, and I begin to fall one last time.

3

I feel rain first, but I'm inside. I look up to see a large collapsed roof. Beams of sunlight shine through its holes, raindrops cascading in a beautiful shimmer. As I walk through decrepit wooden hallways, I realize I'm in an abandoned mansion. I'm surprised by the vastness of the space surrounding me, its intricate Japanese-style joinery a remnant of its former wealth.

A large swimming pool catches my attention, but rather than water it's filled with dirt. Large stalks sprouting from the pool's surface are intertwined with trees bearing bulbous green and yellow fruits at their center. As I look closer, I'm startled to see a little girl. She looks disheveled, her jet-black hair tangled in the debris around her. She's alone, and persistently picking at the ground; perhaps she's plucking weeds. I continue to stare, my mind beginning to wander, until I notice the muffled sounds of Mandarin echoing off the walls of bamboo and mud.

I instinctively walk toward the familiar sound and turn a corner to arrive in a small, cramped space. Its corners are buried, obscured by sleeping mats, metal trinkets, pots, a military uniform, a bucket of water. There's a small wooden table in the center, surrounded by five young boys, all sitting cross-legged on the dirt ground. A woman I don't recognize is carrying a worn bamboo steamer toward the table. She beckons me with little uncertainty, as if she were awaiting my arrival. I join the boys at the table, noticing the tatters in their clothes like the roof and walls around them. She opens the lid to reveal a small whole fish, its plume of aromatic steam filling and familiar.

The boys are ravenous, digging at the center fillet with their chopsticks. The mother picks at the edges around the bones, scraping tender flakes of the remaining fish into one perfect bite. Just as quickly as the fish arrives, the boys and the mother depart, leaving me with just a skeleton on a dirty plate.

I sit in silence, my mind wandering to all the dinners of my past, until I'm startled to find Antoni walking through the doorway with the disheveled little girl who looks no more than eight years old. My heart stops as I look into her eyes. Despite the sadness that gazes back at me, I see a familiar softness—a perpetual smile. The eyes of my grandma.

She rarely spoke of her childhood. I knew her father was a decorated military general in China, and that he and his two wives fled from China to Taiwan in the early 1940s to escape Communism during a civil war. She mentioned she was the youngest in her family, with many older brothers. But this little girl, a face covered in dirt, a soiled rag hanging from her side, an abandoned child, was never what I could've imagined.

I watch as Antoni leads her to the table, a skeleton waiting to greet them. He takes a pair of chopsticks and goes straight for the fish head. He flicks at the cheek, moving the skin away to reveal the most tender white meat. He hands my grandma the chopsticks and she picks off flakes of meat, savoring each little morsel with surprise. She squirms as Antoni uses his fingers to pluck out the eyeballs, popping one straight into his mouth with glee. He hands her the other one, her hunger instinctively accepting it over her better judgment. She puts the eyeball in her mouth, her eyes squeezing shut as the first bite delivers a subtle crunch. She opens her eyes and looks back at Antoni, cracking a smile.

The dinners of past and present begin to weigh on me like an anchor. Dinners with my family that define my happiest moments. Dinners I've paid for with the casual swipe of a credit card. Dinners at Dairy Queen and then Skyline Chili, in that order, just for the hell of it. Dinners where I ask my mom what's for dinner, and she responds, "Anything you want." A world of opportunity, paved by the decisions, sacrifice, and resilience of generations of women before me. My face feels damp. I feel a swell of emotion begin to overwhelm me as Antoni continues to point out to my grandma the various parts of the fish head: the cheeks, the top of the head, the eye sockets, the jowl. I look at God for the first time with gratitude. He gives me a wink, and I wake up.

A steamer—a simple basket designed to capture the latent heat of vaporization—is mighty, and steaming a method that brings out the essence of an ingredient without being fussy. Watching my grandma cook with a steamer feels like watching LeBron on the court in his natural element. She uses a steamer to cook almost everything, from large cuts of meat to whole fish, from vegetables to eggs, you name it. One dish I've learned from her is this steamed chicken. It's cooked simply, with just a subtle marinade to soak into the meat. As it finishes cooking, the tender chicken, steamed in its own juices, becomes a canvas for my grandma's scallion and soy relish. The relish is equal parts sweet and salty, with generous amounts of scallion, ginger, and garlic and a kick of vinegar acidity. It's perfect to eat with rice, to soak up every morsel of flavor.

STEAMED CHICKEN WITH SCALLION AND SOY RELISH

MARINATE THE CHICKEN: In a small mixing bowl, whisk together the Shaoxing wine, soy sauce, and a few grinds of pepper. Place the chicken in a large shallow dish and pour the marinade over. Toss to coat. Cover and let sit in the fridge for 15 to 20 minutes.

STEAM THE CHICKEN: Fill a pot or pan that will fit a bamboo or metal steamer with an inch of water and bring to a boil. Transfer the marinated chicken to a plate that will fit in your steamer, then place the plate into the steamer, making sure it's not completely covering all the steamer holes. (If you can't fit all the chicken on one plate, use two plates and stack your steamers or cook in batches.) Cover and steam the chicken for 15 minutes, until cooked through.

MAKE THE SAUCE: While the chicken steams, in a small saucepan over medium heat, warm the oil. Add the ginger and scallions, and lightly sauté for 30 seconds to 1 minute, until fragrant. Reduce the heat to low and add the honey, soy sauce, vinegar, and water. Continue to cook, stirring, until combined. Set aside.

ASSEMBLE THE DISH: Once the chicken has steamed, remove it from the pot and let it rest in the steamer for 10 minutes. Slice the chicken into thick even slices and place on a serving plate. Spoon the sauce all over the chicken, then top with flaky salt, red pepper flakes, and shiso or basil. Serve with white rice.

MARINADE

2 tablespoons Shaoxing wine or sake

1 tablespoon soy sauce

Freshly ground black pepper

CHICKEN

2 to 2½ pounds boneless, skinless chicken thighs

SAUCE

1 tablespoon canola oil or vegetable oil

1 teaspoon grated fresh ginger

3 scallions, green and white parts, chopped

3 teaspoons honey

2 tablespoons soy sauce

½ teaspoon white vinegar

½ cup water

TOPPINGS

Flaky salt

Red pepper flakes

Chopped shiso or basil

Cooked white rice for serving

Makes 4 servings

Tender salmon is one of those tasty kitchen wins—it delivers so much satisfaction without being difficult. This dish is perfect for throwing together on a whim; its juiciness and flavor all come together in the oven as the salmon roasts in a marinade of soy sauce and fresh orange. The result is a meal full of umami, salt, and sweet acidity.

ROASTED SALMON WITH SOY-ORANGE GLAZE

PREPARE THE FISH: Preheat the oven to 400°F. Season the fish on both sides with a drizzle of olive oil and sprinkles of salt and pepper. Line a baking sheet with parchment paper and place the fish on it.

PREPARE THE SAUCE: In a medium mixing bowl, combine the soy sauce, honey, olive oil, ginger, and apple cider vinegar. Squeeze the juice from the orange half into the bowl. Stir to combine and set aside.

In a medium saucepan over medium heat, melt the butter. Add 4 sprigs of thyme and the garlic to the pan. Sauté for 1 minute, stirring to infuse the butter with flavor. Add the orange slices and onion rings to the pan and cook until the onions have softened slightly and are semitranslucent, about 5 minutes. Stir in the soy sauce mixture and cook for another couple minutes for all the ingredients to get to know each other. Set aside.

COOK THE FISH: Remove the thyme sprigs from the sauce and pour the sauce over the fish on the baking sheet. Strip the leaves from the remaining 2 sprigs of thyme and sprinkle them over the fish. Roast the fish for 12 minutes, until cooked through.

Transfer the fish, onions, and oranges to a serving plate and spoon the remaining sauce from the baking sheet on top. Sprinkle with a little flaky salt and a squeeze of lemon, then top with scallions and sesame seeds to serve.

FISH

One 2-pound piece of Atlantic salmon or steelhead trout

Olive oil

Kosher salt and freshly ground black pepper

SAUCE

1 tablespoon soy sauce

2 tablespoons honey

1 tablespoon olive oil

2 teaspoons grated fresh ginger

1 tablespoon apple cider vinegar

1 medium orange, halved, one half cut into thin slices, the other half left whole

3 tablespoons unsalted butter

6 sprigs thyme

4 garlic cloves, smashed

1 small red onion, thinly sliced into rings

TOPPINGS

Flaky salt

Lemon wedges

Chopped scallions

Sesame seeds

Makes 4 servings

COCA-COLA AND SOY-GLAZED BABY BACK RIBS

My grandma always prepared ribs slow cooked in a simple daikon broth, with ribs sawed into thirds by the butcher and cut between the bone into bite-sized nuggets, a distinct preparation I've only seen in Asian cuisine. My dad meanwhile loved to cook chicken drumsticks in Coca-Cola, balancing the intense sweetness of his favorite soft drink with the saltiness of soy and the acid of vinegar. This recipe uses baby back ribs butchered like my grandma's while braised in my dad's go-to marinade. Just go to your local grocery store and ask the butcher to cut the rack into thirds across the bone to make three long strips. The ribs are slow cooked for a couple hours, its fat rendering in a soy sauce, Coke, and black vinegar marinade, creating a complex sauce that transcends its simple ingredients. The black vinegar meanwhile tenderizes the ribs for fall-off-the-bone bites coated in sweet and salty stickiness. This dish goes great with a simple bowl of white rice, the perfect landing spot to take on all those extra drippings from the ribs.

DRY RUB

2 tablespoons light brown sugar

2 tablespoons granulated sugar

2 teaspoons sweet paprika

1 tablespoon plus 1 teaspoon kosher salt

1 teaspoon onion powder

1 teaspoon freshly ground black pepper

1 teaspoon chopped fresh rosemary

1 tablespoon grated garlic (6 cloves)

¼ teaspoon grated fresh ginger

Makes 4 servings

RIBS

1 full rack baby back ribs, cut into thirds across the bone

MARINADE

2 tablespoons soy sauce

2 teaspoons honey

2 teaspoons black vinegar

1 cup Coca-Cola

TOPPINGS AND ACCOMPANIMENTS

Chopped scallions

1 recipe White Rice (page 102)

PREP THE DRY RUB AND RIBS: In a large mixing bowl, combine the brown sugar, granulated sugar, paprika, salt, onion powder, pepper, rosemary, garlic, and ginger, and stir to mix well.

Chop the baby back ribs into individual pieces by cutting between each bone. Add the baby back ribs to the bowl of dry rub and massage each piece of meat with the dry rub. Cover the bowl and transfer to the fridge for 30 minutes.

COOK THE RIBS: Preheat the oven to 275°F. In a large oven-safe pot or Dutch oven, combine the soy sauce, honey, black vinegar, and Coca-Cola. Add the ribs to the pot and toss them in the marinade, then place the pot into the oven. Roast for 2½ hours, until the ribs are tender and falling off the bone.

GLAZE AND SERVE THE RIBS: Remove the ribs from the oven. Transfer to a serving bowl, top with scallions, and enjoy with a side of white rice.

FAMILY STYLE

This dish will probably make my ancestors pass out, but I just couldn't help myself. Lion's head meatballs are an iconic dish originating in eastern China that has since spread to all parts of China and Taiwan. Large pork meatballs traditionally stewed or steamed in a casserole dish, they absorb the flavors of their own juices and the surrounding napa cabbage like a sponge. I grew up eating lion's head meatballs with rice, but as a kid with a vast imagination and a craving for McDonald's, I always noted the meatballs' similarity to the burger patties in my beloved Big Macs. This recipe is a dream-turned-reality for kid Frankie, a dish that probably shouldn't exist outside of my own brain but has become my own guilty pleasure. It's really a love note to the suburban Midwest seen through the lens of my heritage—a dish that embraces the two parts of my identity that I hid from each other. Divided no more, here they are brought together on one plate in the form of Lion's Head Big Macs.

LION'S HEAD BIG MACS

MAKE THE SCALLION GINGER WATER: In a blender, blend together the water, scallions, and ginger. Strain through a fine-mesh metal sieve and set the liquid aside.

MAKE THE MEAT PATTIES: Chop the ground pork until the texture becomes finer and fluffier. In a large mixing bowl, combine the pork, 4 tablespoons of the scallion ginger water, the Shaoxing wine, soy sauce, sugar, and salt. Mix with your hands until the mixture is well incorporated and sticky. Mix in the egg whites. In a small mixing bowl, whisk 2 tablespoons of the cornstarch and the chicken stock together, and add it to the meat mixture. Mix with your hands to incorporate everything (you can even pick up the mixture and throw it back down into the bowl to create the optimal texture). Cover the bowl and let it sit in the fridge for 30 minutes.

MAKE THE SAUCE: In a small mixing bowl, whisk together the mayonnaise, ketchup, mustard, relish, honey, vinegar, and chili pepper sauce to combine.

SHAPE AND COOK THE PATTIES: In a medium mixing bowl, dissolve the remaining 3 tablespoons cornstarch in 5 tablespoons of water. In a large skillet over medium-high heat, warm 1 tablespoon oil. Dip your hands into the cornstarch water and with wet hands form the meat mixture into 6 patties, tossing the meat between your hands to coat evenly with the cornstarch. Flatten the patties and place them directly on the hot skillet. Cook the patties in batches as needed, pan-frying each side for 4 to 5 minutes until the internal temperature reaches 160°F.

ASSEMBLE THE SANDWICHES: Place one meat patty onto the bottom half of a bun. Top the patty with a slice of cheese and then pickles, onions, and cabbage. Spread some sauce onto the top half of the bun and place over the meat patty and toppings. Repeat for the remaining patties and buns, and serve immediately.

SCALLION GINGER WATER

1 cup water

6 scallions, green and white parts, chopped

1 thumb-sized slice ginger, peeled

MEAT PATTIES

2 pounds ground pork

4 tablespoons scallion ginger water (see above)

2 tablespoons Shaoxing wine or sherry

2 tablespoons soy sauce

2 teaspoons light brown sugar or granulated sugar

1 teaspoon kosher salt

2 egg whites, beaten until frothy and opaque

5 tablespoons cornstarch

1/2 cup chicken stock

Canola oil or vegetable oil

SAUCE

3 tablespoons mayonnaise

2 1/2 teaspoons ketchup

1/2 teaspoon yellow mustard

2 teaspoons sweet pickle relish

1/2 teaspoon honey

1/2 teaspoon white wine vinegar

1/2 teaspoon chili pepper sauce (like Sriracha)

BUNS

6 hamburger buns, halved

TOPPINGS

Sliced cheddar cheese

Cold Marinated Pickles (page 22)

Sliced white onion

Napa cabbage leaves

Makes 6 sandwiches

MOM'S TOMATO SEAFOOD STEW

This is my mom's dish, a warm stew that came together during the long weeks when I was in school and both she and my dad worked. She tells me that this stew came about from pulling leftover ingredients from the fridge. Tomatoes from stir-fried tomato egg dishes; extra onions and carrots from other stir-fries. It starts with the acidity of raw tomatoes, which simmer and transform into a sweetness that circulates throughout the broth. Fresh fish and shrimp anchor the stew to the ocean, the chunks of white and pink adding flavor in the final moments of cooking. It's best enjoyed with a bowl of simple white rice, every grain soaking in flavor.

Olive oil

10 garlic cloves, smashed

2 sweet onions, chopped

½ cup Shaoxing wine

4 cups chicken bone broth

½ teaspoon minced ginger plus 4 thumb-sized slices ginger

3 medium carrots, chopped

6 medium tomatoes, quartered

1 tablespoon light brown sugar

1 tablespoon kosher salt

1 bay leaf

1 pound shrimp, peeled and deveined

1 pound halibut or other whitefish, skinned and cut into 1-inch chunks

Chopped scallions for garnish

Chopped cilantro for garnish

Cooked white rice or noodles for serving

Makes 6 servings

In a large pot or Dutch oven over medium-high heat, warm a generous glug of olive oil. Add the garlic and cook for 1 minute, until fragrant and sizzling. Toss in the onions and reduce the heat to low-medium. Cook the onions and garlic for 10 minutes, stirring occasionally, until the onions are soft and translucent. Stir in the Shaoxing wine and let it cook off for about 5 minutes. Pour in the broth and add the ginger, carrots, tomatoes, brown sugar, salt, and bay leaf, and bring to a boil. Reduce the heat to a soft simmer and cook for 1 hour and 20 minutes, until the tomatoes have completely broken down. Add the shrimp and fish to the pot and simmer for 10 minutes, until cooked through. Remove from the heat and add salt to taste. Ladle into serving bowls and top with scallions and cilantro. Serve immediately, with rice or noodles on the side.

When I was growing up, my family never used the oven. The oven mostly served as a glorified pot holder, its real function a complete mystery to me and my grandma. It wasn't until we watched Ina Garten pull a golden-brown roast chicken out of her pot holder that we understood an oven's true purpose. Watching Ina's Food Network show *Barefoot Contessa* was our ritual. Her otherworldly cooking in the fairy-tale setting of the Hamptons was a fantasy my grandma and I could bond over. This recipe invokes another fantasy—a world where Ina Garten and my grandma get to cook together. A whole roasted chicken stuffed with aromatics absorbs my grandma's flavors of chili crisp, scallion, and ginger through a rich glaze poured over its crisp skin.

CHILI CRISP AND HONEY ROASTED WHOLE CHICKEN

BRINE THE CHICKEN: Very generously sprinkle kosher salt (about 1 teaspoon per pound) on the whole chicken from front to back and inside the cavity. Let it rest at room temperature for 30 minutes.

While the chicken rests, place 10 of the scallions, the 2 tablespoons salt, ground ginger, sugar, rice vinegar, and water in a blender and blend until smooth. Once the chicken is ready, place in a gallon-size zip-top bag. Pour the blended scallion brine into the bag and seal. Refrigerate for 24 hours, flipping it around the halfway mark so the chicken brines evenly.

STUFF THE CHICKEN: The next day, preheat the oven to 425°F. Line a baking sheet with aluminum foil. Remove the chicken from the plastic bag and gently wipe off the excess brine. Tuck the garlic, fresh ginger, and remaining 4 scallions into the cavity.

Place the chicken on the prepared baking sheet, breast side up. Tie the legs together with kitchen string and tuck the wing tips under the body of the chicken. Melt the 2 tablespoons butter and brush an even layer all over the chicken. Roast at 425°F for 30 minutes. Reduce the heat to 400°F and roast for another 35 to 40 minutes, until the internal temperature is 165°F or the juices run clear.

MAKE THE SAUCE: While the chicken roasts, in a small pot over medium heat, melt the 4 tablespoons butter. Add the vinegar, honey, soy sauce, chili crisp, and rosemary, and stir until incorporated and smooth. Bring to a simmer, then pour into a container and set aside.

CARVE AND SERVE THE CHICKEN: When the chicken is done, remove it from the oven, cover it with foil, and let rest 15 to 20 minutes. Uncover and carve into breasts (slice breasts into 4 or 5 pieces for easier sharing), thighs, drumsticks, and wings, and place onto a platter. Pour the sauce over the chicken and top with scallions and cilantro to serve.

CHICKEN

2 tablespoons kosher salt, plus more for sprinkling

One 4- to 5-pound chicken

14 scallions, with ends trimmed

1 tablespoon ground ginger

1 tablespoon granulated sugar

4 teaspoons of rice vinegar or lemon juice

2 cups water

1 garlic head, halved

1 thumb-sized slice ginger

2 tablespoons unsalted butter

SAUCE

4 tablespoons unsalted butter

2 tablespoons apple cider vinegar

¼ cup plus 1 tablespoon honey

3 tablespoons soy sauce

1 tablespoon chili crisp

1½ teaspoons chopped fresh rosemary (from 1 sprig)

TOPPINGS

Chopped scallions

Chopped cilantro

Makes 3 to 4 servings

WHOLE STEAMED FISH

清蒸魚

This dish, very dear to my heart and my stomach, is a family meal that's been present at the table for many generations before me. It always starts with a trip to the Asian supermarket, where my grandma chooses the perfect live fish from amongst a sea of its friends in a tank. I always feel bad for the chosen one, usually offering up a little prayer in which I say sorry to the little guy. My pity is soon superseded by gratefulness for its tasty sacrifice, knowing my grandma will treat the fish well. Back at home, she marinates the whole fish in a drizzle of rice wine (which she says removes the fishy smell) and soy sauce (which adds salt and color). Slivers of ginger are placed in the cavity and on top of the fish, and it's steamed until completely tender. Once it's cooked, a pile of julienned scallions adds freshness to the fish's gentle taste. The final touch is a pour of hot oil over the top, providing an additional flash-fry of aromatic flavor as the oil sizzles over the scallions and ginger and drips onto the tender fish. We dig into the fish with chopsticks, navigating around the bones to savor every tender morsel.

One 1½- to 2-pound whole tilapia, snapper, or striped sea bass, cleaned and scaled

1 teaspoon kosher salt

1 tablespoon Shaoxing wine or sake

½ tablespoon soy sauce

½ teaspoon honey

½ tablespoon water

2 thumb-sized knobs of ginger, peeled and thinly sliced lengthwise

4 scallions, green and white parts

3 tablespoons grapeseed oil, peanut oil, or vegetable oil

Makes 4 servings

Tip:
If you don't have an Asian supermarket near you, look for a whole fish at your local fishmonger or supermarket, and have them scale and clean it for you.

PREP THE FISH: With kitchen shears, remove the fins on the sides and bottom of the fish. With a knife, scrape against the fish to remove any scales that still remain. Rinse the fish with cold water and pat dry. Starting just behind the fin, cut three parallel lines diagonally across the fish then place onto a heatproof plate. Season the fish with the salt. Pour the Shaoxing wine on both sides of the fish. Mix together the soy sauce, honey, and water in a bowl, and then pour on both sides of the fish.

PREP THE AROMATICS: Stack a few ginger slices at a time and cut into thin strips. Repeat until all the ginger has been cut. Place half the ginger strips into the cavity of the fish and the other half on top of the fish. Slice the scallions into thirds crosswise, then cut lengthwise into long, thin strips; set aside. Place the plate of fish into a bamboo steamer. If you don't have a bamboo steamer, place the plate on a metal steamer basket and put a lid on the pot to cover. If the fish doesn't fit on the plate, cut the tail and place it next to the fish.

STEAM THE FISH: Fill a pot that will fit your steamer with an inch of water and bring to a boil. Place the steamer in the pot and cover. Steam for 10 minutes, until the fish is tender but not flaky and overcooked. The fish's eyes will be completely opaque when it's ready. Sprinkle the scallion strips all over the top of the fish and continue steaming, covered, for 2 minutes.

ASSEMBLE THE DISH: In a small skillet over high heat, warm the oil until it's very hot (it will be glistening). Remove from the heat and carefully pour all over the scallion strips atop the fish; it will sizzle. Serve immediately.

Eating hot pot is like the perfect spa day. You'll start with an aromatic facial from a slow-simmering chicken broth. Breathe in and relax as its plumes of steam fill every pore of your skin with ginger and the savory scent of tender meat. Your face will glisten as if you've been sprayed with Chanel N° Chicken parfum; you'll have never looked better. You'll proceed to the sauna next. It's a dining room filled with a pleasant humidity and your sweaty loved ones. They sit at a circular table filled like a map. An array of sliced meats crowds one end of the table—strips of pork butt and marbled beef their own red country. Chrysanthemum greens and mushrooms of all sizes spill out of bowls like an overgrown forest. Little islands of peanut sauces, sacha barbecue sauce, and soy and scallion marinade all dot the remaining table landscape. At the center is a hot plate topped with a welcoming pot of simmering chicken broth—a communal bath not for you and your family members (thank God) but for raw ingredients to soak in. As the ritual of hot pot commences, the dining room fills with steam. Every dunk of fatty meat or earthy vegetable leaves behind the gift of its own unique aroma, transforming a simple broth into an intense concentration of flavor as it cooks.

The bowl in front of you houses an endless cycle of dishes of your own making. A scoop of tofu and tender napa cabbage leaves sitting in spoonfuls of broth become a light soup to ease into the meal. A pile of pea shoots blanched in the hot pot are tossed with soy and scallion sauce to become a hearty vegetarian dish with a salty-sweet crunch. Thin slabs of tender pork belly swimming with chewy noodles are drizzled with a slot machine of sauces, from garlic peanut to chili crisp, transforming your bowl into an all-you-can-eat noodle bar.

You'll never feel so hot, relaxed, and full at the same time; it's a lethal combination scientists like to call postprandial somnolence, also known as a food coma. I like to think of it as a state of bliss. A body's natural response to a shared activity filled with the generosity of endless flavors and conversation amongst family, all profusely sweating together at the table for the love of food.

Hot Pot

How to Hot Pot

Hot pot is a meal centered around the joy of cooking raw ingredients in a simmering pot of stock at the table with friends and family. Anyone at the table can freely toss ingredients into the broth to cook and eat, crafting their own flavors and dishes with a mix of cooked foods and dipping sauces. Every family has its own style of hot pot; the preparation below is just one version of the many regional varieties that exist today.

What You'll Need

HOT PLATE — A hot plate or portable gas burner keeps broth simmering at the center of the table.

MESH STRAINERS — 3-inch metal strainers that are perfect for scooping ingredients from the hot pot after cooking while leaving excess broth behind.

CHOPSTICKS — Use these to easily place ingredients into the hot pot and fetch anything cooked that looks tasty.

Enjoying Hot Pot

Place all the other ingredients into separate bowls/on separate plates, putting each category of ingredients (meat, vegetables, etc.) together. Place them all around the hot pot. Give each person a bowl and either a mesh strainer or chopsticks to fetch ingredients.

Pour the stock into a wide, shallow pot and set it on the hot plate. Turn the heat to high and bring to a medium simmer. Lower the temperature to maintain this simmer, adjusting the heat when cooking as needed to keep it at a simmer, and adding more stock or water as necessary.

When the stock is simmering, feel free to open up the table to add ingredients. My family likes to start with vegetables first and move onto meats, but the order is totally up to personal preference.

When cooking meats, wait to scoop up any other vegetables or other cooked items that remain in the hot pot until all the meat is cooked through. Enjoy any combination of meats, vegetables, and noodles with sauces or stock.

Napa cabbage leaves   FIG. 01

Baby bok choy   FIG. 04

King trumpet mushroom   FIG. 07

Chrysanthemum leaves   FIG. 02

Beech mushroom   FIG. 05

Sliced pork butt   FIG. 08

Pea shoots   FIG. 03

Bunapi mushroom   FIG. 06

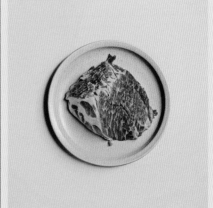

Sliced fatty beef   FIG. 09

Sliced pork belly   **FIG. 10**

Meatballs   **FIG. 13**

Soy and scallion sauce   **FIG. 16**

Fried tofu   **FIG. 11**

Taro   **FIG. 14**

Chili crisp   **FIG. 17**

Firm tofu   **FIG. 12**

Vermicelli noodles   **FIG. 15**

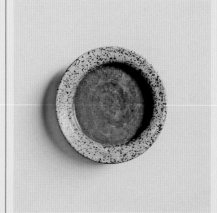

Creamy peanut sauce   **FIG. 18**

STOCK

Any simple stock, whether store-bought or homemade, is sufficient for hot pot, as it will take on even more flavor over time as raw ingredients continue to simmer in the liquid. Every family has their own traditions, but my family prefers to keep it simple by making an easy stock like my Simple Vegetable Stock (page 13). I like to have about 2 to 3 quarts of stock for 4 to 6 people.

Chicken stock (page 12)

Vegetable stock (page 13)

LEAFY GREENS

Any variety of leafy greens can be blanched or cooked through, but heartier greens such as kale or napa cabbage are perfect for hot pot as they can withstand the rolling simmer of a stock without becoming mushy. A trip to the Asian supermarket will gift you with flavorful greens not found in American grocery stores. My personal favorite are pea shoot vines, their fat stems and crunchy tendrils so full of crisp flavor. My family also loves to get chrysanthemum greens, whose garland of serrated leaves need only a quick blanch to offer an herbaceous and sweet crunch. I typically like to grab around 1/2 to 3/4 pound of greens from the Asian market to easily satisfy a group of 4.

Napa cabbage leaves

Kale

Pea shoot vines

Chrysanthemum leaves

Baby bok choy

MUSHROOMS

I like to get around a 1/2 pound of different sizes and flavors of mushrooms for 4 people, but there's no wrong way to choose mushrooms, as they are all delicious sponges of flavor and texture. Thin enoki mushrooms are delightful; they remind me of little strands of noodles. King oyster mushrooms, also a highlight for their robust meatiness, are best enjoyed when cut into thick slices.

Shiitake mushrooms

Enoki mushrooms

King oyster (king trumpet) mushrooms

Bunapi mushrooms

Beech mushrooms

SLICED MEATS

Meats for hot pot are typically prepared thinly sliced so they can be enjoyed within a couple minutes of being dunked in simmering broth. I recommend going to an Asian supermarket to buy meat, as they tend to have it prepackaged and thinly sliced specifically for hot pot, making prep much simpler. I tend to buy 2 1/2 to 3 pounds of meat when preparing hot pot for 4 people.

Sliced pork butt

Sliced pork belly

Sliced fatty beef, such as brisket or ribeye

Sliced boneless chicken thighs or breasts

SEAFOOD

Seafood makes a great addition to hot pot as it cooks quite quickly. My family has always had a plate of thick slices of salmon ready for a quick 2-minute dunk in a mesh strainer. Shell-on shrimp also works well, absorbing all the flavors of the stock and cooked ingredients for a moist, succulent bite.

Scallops

Shrimp

Sliced fish (salmon is my personal favorite)

MEATBALLS

Asian supermarket meatballs are a delight to eat. They come prepackaged in a variety of flavors such as beef, fish, chicken, and pork, and have the most satisfyingly chewy QQ texture. If you'd like to make your own, all the dumpling fillings in Chapter 5 work well rolled into hot pot meatballs. A tip I learned from my aunt and uncle to get that familiar chewy meatball texture is to freeze the meat mixture first, then slice it into smaller pieces when it's slightly defrosted but still feels like a popsicle. Next, blend the meat in a food processor until extremely smooth, then form into meatballs and cook in the hot pot.

Pork meatballs

Chicken meatballs

Fish meatballs

Beef meatballs

TOFU

All tofu varieties are highly efficient vehicles for absorbing flavor from the hot pot. Fried tofu, a personal favorite with its chewy outer skin and soft inside, holds up well in the simmering stock. For firm tofu, my uncle taught me a little trick where the tofu is pre cut into cubes and frozen the night before. This allows it to withstand the simmering water while become chewier and more absorbent of flavor.

Fried tofu

Firm Tofu

NOODLES

I personally love noodles in hot pot, as they provide a nice base for the meat, vegetables, and stock, but they can be completely optional if you want to optimize for other ingredients. I find that 1 pound of noodles should be more than sufficient for 4 people when eaten with everything else.

Fresh flour noodles

Vermicelli noodles

Rice cakes

STARCHES

Starches are the lovely carb break in hot pot that no one asked for (because they're already so full from everything else) but that everyone in my family enjoys. I usually will get around ½ to 1 pound of starches depending on how hungry I'm feeling. I peel and slice these thickly, as they become quite soft when boiled. For taro, my aunt taught me to roast thick slices in advance at 375°F for 20 minutes, flipping halfway, so that when they boil in the hot pot, they retain their smooth, soft texture without falling apart.

Butternut squash

Taro

Sweet potato

SAUCES AND AROMATICS

Dipping sauces are a key part of the hot pot experience. These condiments allow for personalization in flavor for the many ingredients that get scooped up from the hot pot. I like to have two or three sauces on the table, along with small dishes of freshly chopped aromatics.

Soy and Scallion Sauce (page 11)

Spicy Soy and Scallion Sauce (page 11)

Chili crisp

Peanut sauce (page 12)

Sacha sauce (A savory Chinese barbecue sauce made with oil, garlic, shallots, chili, dried shrimp, and Chinese brill)

Toasted sesame oil

Minced garlic

Chopped scallions

Chopped cilantro

BAKE SALE

the perfect childhood menu if given free rein and his parents had amnesia, written by thirteen-year-old Frankie to his younger self

BREAKFAST
Cinnamon Toast Crunch

To start the day, eat Cinnamon Toast Crunch in exactly the following order: Start by pouring cold milk in the bowl first. This step is important, despite your friends thinking you're a total psychopath. They'll tell you it's the equivalent of putting dressing into a bowl before your salad greens. They'll tell you that 95 percent of the population puts cereal in the bowl before milk, which may be true, but don't give in. Have the entire bag of Cinnamon Toast Crunch within arm's reach. Pour *only* the amount you'll eat in one or two spoonfuls, and eat the cereal. Once it's gone, pour a couple more spoonfuls into the bowl. Repeat until you're full or the milk is gone. You've now just had the crunchiest cereal bowl of your life while everyone else continues to eat spoonful after spoonful of soggy mush. Who's the psychopath now?

LUNCH
Keebler Sandies and Cap'n Crunch

Here's the deal. The school cafeteria is like the Met Gala of processed food, an arena of hormonal teenagers parading the finest accoutrements Walmart has to offer. Yes, I realize you have Asian parents. They're not well versed in the language of Gushers or the nuances of Lunchables pizza. Your mom might even, God forbid, give in to her motherly instincts and give you your favorite Asian fruit jelly cups or a couple Yakults. DON'T LET HER. You've worked hard to establish your dominance as king of the lunch box. You've refined the weekly Friday reveal of Panera's Frontega Chicken sandwich, making everyone else's bologna-and-cheese look like a sad pile of poo. However, if it's high season—Chinese New Year, a new zodiac year, an annual "we're not a racist school so let's dress up all your white classmates in different ethnicities" day (also known as Culture Day), all of which will bring attention to your Asian-ness—proceed with the following: Pack a large bag of Cap'n Crunch and a carton of milk. Seems basic, but breakfast for lunch is a surprising tactic they won't see coming. Even those white kids' Fruit Roll-Up–packing, Go-GURT–slinging parents wouldn't have the audacity to put 40 percent of their child's recommended daily sugar intake into a single lunch. But you're not finished. Take out an entire package of Keebler Sandies and crush those shortbread pecan cookies into chunks, sprinkling them in your bowl of Cap'n Crunch and milk. Take a hearty spoonful, enjoy the deliciousness, and bask in the awe radiating from your classmates.

DINNER
Black Sesame Candy and Butter Mochi

It's a full-time job having to pretend you're not Asian. You're home now. Relax, shed that L.L. Bean bag, and slip on those plastic Asian house slippers. You'll have a few hours to wind down before both your parents come home from work. Grab a handful of that candy your parents got from Cam's Asian Market, and cop a squat on the carpet. Turn the TV on; the *Maury* show is on Channel 3. Let the screams of "You are not the father!" and the crunch of black sesame candy soothe you. The candy will hold you over during dinner. Dinner is tricky because your mom's main priority is that you grow to be six feet tall. This is evidenced by the obscene amounts of broccoli you are fed, the closest you can probably get to eating a human fart. Your mom also has resorted to pulling on your legs before bed every night to "increase your height" because you refuse to play basketball. This is a tolerable compromise, as your DNA and sweet tooth have blessed you with the plumpness of a peach and the athleticism of a beached whale. Once you've "eaten" your dinner, you'll still be hungry because you've most likely chewed the broccoli, held it in your mouth, then proceeded to spit it all out in the toilet when you "went to pee." For your real dinner, find the butter mochi your mom picked up from Linda at Chinese school last Sunday. Look for a Tupperware container that holds an object swaddled in twenty layers of plastic wrap, like a bundle of cocaine. Of all the cereals, cookies, and desserts you love, nothing beats the first bite of an Asian mom's chewy, homemade butter mochi—a delicious dinner indeed.

BLACK SESAME CARAMEL AND CHOCOLATE CHIP COOKIES

Salted black sesame caramel is the star of these chocolate chip cookies. The recipe begins with making a caramel on the stove, the miracle of water and melting sugar transforming into a complex nuttiness. Next, black sesame seeds are ground into a powder and then folded into the amber caramel along with butter, heavy cream, and some salt, creating a sticky mixture that takes me back to the ooziness of black sesame tang yuan (sweet glutinous rice balls) on Chinese New Year. The salted black sesame caramel is then mixed into chocolate chip cookie dough, for the ultimate Asian American treat.

BLACK SESAME CARAMEL

½ cup black sesame seeds

1 cup granulated sugar

3 tablespoons water

½ teaspoon fresh lemon juice

½ cup heavy cream

4 tablespoons unsalted butter, at room temperature

2 teaspoons kosher salt

COOKIE DOUGH

2 cups all-purpose flour

½ teaspoon baking soda

2 teaspoons kosher salt

8 tablespoons unsalted butter, at room temperature

1 cup granulated sugar

¼ cup light brown sugar

2 teaspoons vanilla extract

1 egg

3½ ounces dark chocolate, chopped

Flaky salt for sprinkling

Makes 8 large cookies

MAKE THE BLACK SESAME CARAMEL: Line a baking sheet with parchment paper. In a coffee grinder or food processor, grind the black sesame seeds into a fine powder. If you don't have an appliance to grind the seeds, put them in a zip-top bag and roll over them with a rolling pin to crush them.

In a medium pot, combine the sugar, water, and lemon juice (the lemon juice helps prevent crystallization), and cook over medium heat for 8 minutes (don't touch, just let it do its thing). As brown spots start to appear around the edges, occasionally swirl the pot to distribute the sugar evenly as it reaches caramelization.

Once the mixture is amber and smells nutty, remove from heat. Carefully pour in the heavy cream and stir vigorously, being careful to not burn your hands on the geyser of steam. Add the butter and mix until incorporated. Mix in the kosher salt and ground black sesame powder and stir until it becomes a smooth black caramel. Return the pot to the heat and cook over medium until the caramel reaches 260°F on a candy thermometer. Pour the caramel onto the prepared baking sheet and let cool and thicken while you make the dough.

MAKE THE COOKIE DOUGH: Preheat the oven to 350°F. Line 2 baking sheets with aluminum foil. In a medium mixing bowl, mix together the flour, baking soda, and kosher salt. In a large mixing bowl using a hand mixer or in the bowl of a stand mixer fitted with a paddle attachment, beat the butter until light and fluffy. Add the granulated and brown sugars and mix until smooth. Add the vanilla and egg and mix until smooth. Add the flour mixture to the butter mixture a little bit at a time until it's fully incorporated. Chop half of the cooled black sesame caramel (save the other half to eat by itself) and add to the dough along with the chopped chocolate. Mix roughly with a spatula.

BAKE THE COOKIES: Scoop ⅓ cup of dough using a cup measure and form into a ball. Place 4 balls onto one of the baking sheets, evenly spaced apart, then top each one with a sprinkle of flaky salt. Place the baking sheet into the freezer for 10 minutes. When ready, bake for 16 minutes, until the dough has spread and the cookie edges are crisp, with slightly gooey centers. (As you're baking the first batch, place the second baking sheet in the freezer.) Repeat for the second batch.

Transfer the cookies to a wire rack and make sure they cool down completely before removing (if you try to eat them right away, they'll be too soft and will break). Remove from the baking sheet and dig in.

I love how the tradition of mochi spans memories and cultures, from Filipino bibingka and Chinese nian gao to Japanese mochi and Hawaiian butter mochi. Mochi's presence in my daily life was fleeting. It was a beloved sweet seen only in the confines of the Asian community my parents were a part of: in a Tupperware from another Chinese mother, an unassuming Styrofoam container by the register of a small Asian grocery store, a Pyrex pan next to bags of Doritos and Lay's on a plastic table at Chinese school. Months could pass before I ate mochi again, but every new taste was a surprise, its many variations—from steamed brown sugar nian gao to orange disks of sweet potato butter mochi—making every bite different from the last.

This recipe combines my memories of mochi with my cravings for my favorite breakfast cereal, Cinnamon Toast Crunch. The batter is made by combining glutinous rice flour with milk soaked in Cinnamon Toast Crunch. (The soaking is a genius method by chef Christina Tosi, while the batter is inspired by Alana Kysar's wonderful butter mochi recipe in *Aloha Kitchen*.) The cinnamon-sugar and cereal-milk batter is then topped with more crushed Cinnamon Toast Crunch and baked into a crisp and chewy nostalgic treat.

CINNAMON TOAST CRUNCH BUTTER MOCHI

SOAK THE CEREAL: In a medium mixing bowl, combine the 2 cups milk or nondairy milk with 2 cups of the Cinnamon Toast Crunch. Let soak for at least 1 hour or up to overnight, covered in the fridge. Strain the milk through a fine-mesh metal sieve; you should get about 1 cup of cereal milk.

MAKE THE BROWN BUTTER: Heat a small saucepan over medium heat. Add 4 tablespoons of the butter and stir frequently as it starts to melt and bubble. Look for little brown specks to start to appear and the color to change from yellow to a light amber, 3 to 5 minutes. Once it's lightly browned, remove from the heat and transfer to a heatproof container to cool.

MIX THE BATTER: Preheat the oven to 350°F. Grease a 9-inch square baking pan or cake pan. In a large mixing bowl, whisk together the eggs, 1 cup cereal milk, the coconut milk, maple syrup, and vanilla until smooth. Add in the Mochiko rice flour, 1 cup of the brown sugar, baking powder, and 1/4 teaspoon of the salt and whisk until it becomes a smooth batter. Pour in the browned butter and continue to mix until incorporated. Pour the batter into the prepared pan.

CRUMBLE, BAKE, AND SERVE: Crush the remaining 3 cups Cinnamon Toast Crunch with your hands until it's a quarter of its original size. Melt the remaining 4 tablespoons butter, then pour it onto the crushed cereal. Mix in the remaining 2 teaspoons brown and sugar and 1/2 teaspoon salt. Top the batter evenly with the crushed cereal mixture.

Bake for 1 hour, until golden brown. You'll know when it's done if you stick a chopstick in it and it comes out clean. Cool completely on a wire rack, then cut into squares, sprinkle with some powdered sugar, cinnamon, and flaky salt, and serve. Store covered and enjoy within 3 days.

2 cups milk or non-dairy milk

5 cups Cinnamon Toast Crunch cereal

8 tablespoons unsalted butter

2 eggs

1 cup coconut milk

2 teaspoons maple syrup

1 teaspoon vanilla extract

2½ cups Mochiko sweet rice flour

1 cup plus 2 teaspoons light brown sugar

1 teaspoon baking powder

3/4 teaspoon kosher salt

Powdered sugar for topping

Ground cinnamon for topping

Flaky salt for topping

Makes 16 squares

CAP'N CRUNCH AND PECAN SHORTBREAD COOKIES

In this recipe, Cap'n Crunch, in all its golden gloriousness, is used to re-create my favorite pecan shortbread cookie, Keebler Sandies. The finely ground cereal is used in the shortbread dough as the foundation for this cookie. The Trojan horse that brings two seemingly disparate inspirations together is miso, its depth of saltiness elevating the flavors of pecan chunks, butter shortbread, and Cap'n Crunch into umami heaven. The shortbread dough is rolled in a mixture of demerara sugar and crushed Cap'n Crunch, then baked to a crisp golden yellow—perfect for a dip in a glass of milk.

3½ cups Cap'n Crunch cereal

1¾ cups all-purpose flour

1 cup (2 sticks) unsalted butter, at room temperature

½ cup granulated sugar

¼ cup light brown sugar

1 teaspoon vanilla extract

1 tablespoon white miso

⅓ cup chopped pecans

½ cup demerara sugar

Flaky salt

Makes 20 cookies

PREP THE DRY INGREDIENTS: In a food processor, finely grind 2 cups of the Cap'n Crunch; you should end up with ¾ cup ground cereal. In a medium mixing bowl, combine the ground cereal with the flour. Set aside.

MAKE THE COOKIE DOUGH: In a large mixing bowl or the bowl of a stand mixer, combine the butter, granulated sugar, brown sugar, vanilla, and miso. Using a hand mixer or the paddle attachment of the stand mixer, beat the mixture on medium-high speed until it's smooth and fluffy, around 3 minutes or so. With the mixer on low speed, slowly incorporate the Cap'n Crunch/flour mixture until combined. Add 1 cup Cap'n Crunch and the chopped pecans, and mix on low speed until incorporated.

MAKE THE DOUGH LOGS: Remove the dough from the mixing bowl and divide it in half. Place one half on a large piece of plastic wrap. Fold the plastic wrap over the dough and roll into a log approximately 2 to 2½ inches in diameter. Repeat with the other dough half, and then place both halves in the fridge and chill for 1 to 2 hours, until completely firm.

SLICE AND BAKE THE DOUGH: Preheat the oven to 350°F. Line two baking sheets with parchment paper. In a small mixing bowl, crush the remaining ½ cup Cap'n Crunch into small pieces. Add the demerara sugar to the bowl and mix to combine. Transfer the mixture to a large plate. Remove the dough from the fridge, unwrap, and brush with water. Roll each log in the Cap'n Crunch/sugar mixture so that it creates a crust. After rolling, slice each log into ½-inch disks and place onto the baking sheets 1 inch apart. Sprinkle with flaky salt and bake for 16 minutes, until cooked through and the edges have browned, swapping the baking sheets at the halfway point so the cookies bake evenly. Transfer the cookies to a wire rack to cool completely, then serve.

Growing up, I never left a checkout lane without a package of Reese's Peanut Butter Cups. I love the good chew of a Snickers bar, and Hershey's Cookies 'n' Creme candy bars are so deliciously decadent, but my heart and stomach will always belong to classic chocolate and peanut butter. I couldn't eat peanut butter cups every day, so convincing my parents that Reese's Puffs cereal was a healthy alternative was the next best thing. Its crunchy balls of chocolate and peanut butter are satisfyingly dessert-like and a perfect component to incorporate into the classic brownie. In this recipe, Reese's Puffs are mixed into the batter (as a finely ground powder) and also star in a delicious crumble topping (blended with butter and sugar) that creates a crisp coating atop the baked brownie.

REESE'S PUFFS BROWNIES

PREP THE PAN: Preheat the oven to 350°F and grease a 9 by 13-inch rectangular pan. (For easier lifting, you can line the pan with aluminum foil, then grease it, leaving extra to hang over the sides.)

MAKE THE BATTER: Heat a medium saucepan over medium heat. Add the butter and mix frequently as it starts to melt and bubble. Look for little brown specks to start to appear and the color to change from yellow to a light amber, 3 to 5 minutes. Once it's lightly browned, remove from the heat and mix in the granulated sugar, vanilla, and semisweet chocolate, stirring to melt the chocolate. Once the chocolate mixture is smooth, pour into a large mixing bowl.

In a food processor, finely grind the Reese's Puffs; you should end up with ½ cup ground cereal. Add to the chocolate mixture. Add the cocoa powder, espresso powder, cinnamon, salt, eggs, and flour. Mix together with a silicone spatula or wooden spoon to get a thick, smooth batter.

MAKE THE CRUMBLE: In a blender, combine the cold butter, flour, brown sugar, and salt. Pulse a few times until you get small chunks the size of peas. Add the Reese's Puffs and pulse again once or twice; you'll have some crushed cereal and some whole pieces.

BAKE THE BROWNIES: Pour the batter into the prepared pan and spread evenly with a spatula. Sprinkle the Reese's Puffs crumble evenly over the top of the batter. Bake for 30 to 35 minutes, until cooked through. (Test doneness by sticking a toothpick in the center of the brownies. If it comes out without any wet batter on it, the brownies are done.) Set the pan on a wire rack to cool completely and have the crumb set. Cut into squares and serve, or store in a sealed container for up to 5 days.

BROWNIE BATTER

10 tablespoons unsalted butter, cut into 1-inch pieces

1½ cups granulated sugar

2 teaspoons vanilla extract

4 ounces semisweet chocolate, chopped

1 cup Reese's Puffs cereal

½ cup Dutch-processed cocoa powder

½ teaspoon espresso powder

1 teaspoon ground cinnamon

1½ teaspoons kosher salt

3 eggs

1 cup all-purpose flour

REESE'S PUFFS CRUMBLE

6 tablespoons cold butter, cut into 1-inch pieces

½ cup all-purpose flour

¾ cup light brown sugar

½ teaspoon kosher salt

1 cup Reese's Puffs cereal

Makes 24 brownies

OOLONG MILK TEA AND ALMOND RICE CRISPY TREATS

It shouldn't be a surprise that I loved Rice Krispies Treats growing up, and still love them to this day. I'm grateful to Mildred Day, their inventor (and patron saint of bake sales everywhere). The simple combination of melted marshmallow coating grains of crisp rice cereal is pure sticky genius. My recipe takes its inspiration from the original confection, but I've added flavors reminiscent of all the Asian treats I had growing up, like the chewy milk candies we ate in my dad's Toyota Previa, their wrappers stamped with rabbits littering the tan felt floor. I'm also transported back to slurping oolong milk tea with boba through fat straws, the liquid's sweet creaminess with hints of earth distinctly satisfying. I love how food can be a bridge of commonalities between any two cultures, and coming up with my own rice crispy treats felt like the perfect medium to express my love for these sweet memories. For these treats, I infuse melted marshmallow with oolong tea, which is then folded into the rice cereal to infuse each grain with creamy earthiness. Sliced almonds are incorporated into the final mixture to provide an extra nuttiness to balance out the oolong and to give a crunchy texture.

Neutral oil

6 cups crispy rice cereal

4 tablespoons butter

One 10-ounce bag mini marshmallows

½ teaspoon vanilla extract

5 to 6 teaspoons finely ground oolong tea

½ cup sliced roasted almonds

Makes 16

PREP THE BOWLS, POTS, AND PAN: Brush a large mixing bowl and a large pot with neutral oil (this will keep the marshmallows from making a big sticky mess). Line a 9-inch square baking pan with parchment paper, leaving extra overhang on each side (this will allow you to pull out the treats from the pan when they're baked). Pour the crispy rice cereal into the large oiled bowl and set aside.

BROWN THE BUTTER AND MELT THE MARSHMALLOWS: In the large oiled pot over medium heat, melt the butter, stirring continuously, until it starts to turn a light brown color, a few minutes or so. Once the butter has lightly browned, turn the heat off and add 4 cups of the marshmallows, the vanilla, and the tea. Continuously stir as the marshmallows melt and form a smooth consistency.

MIX TOGETHER AND SERVE: Working quickly, pour the melted marshmallow into the large mixing bowl of crispy rice cereal, scraping any extra on the sides with a silicone spatula. With a silicone or rubber spatula, stir the cereal and marshmallow together until it's evenly mixed. Add the 1 cup remaining marshmallows and the almonds and continue to mix until evenly distributed. Scoop the mixture into the prepared pan, and with oiled or wet fingers, gently press the mixture into the pan to spread evenly. Let cool completely (about 1 hour), then use the parchment paper to lift the treats out of the pan. Cut into squares to serve, or store in an airtight container for up to 3 days.

If Cinnamon Toast Crunch magically turned into large slices of toast, it would be this recipe. It's a tribute to many a Midwestern kid's food pyramid during breakfast: carbs, maple syrup, and melted butter. As my cravings became sweet while my pubescent hormones made me a raging lunatic, my parents learned to dangle this holy trifecta of a balanced meal in front me alongside a Saturday morning binge of Kids WB cartoons—the ultimate bribe to get all my schoolwork done and make it to the end of the week. This nostalgic recipe uses thick slices of Fluffy Cornmeal White Bread (page 39) with slathers of cinnamon maple butter and sprinkles of walnuts and sesame. If you haven't made the homemade bread, feel free to use store-bought and just make the maple cinnamon butter.

In a small mixing bowl, mix together the butter, maple syrup, cinnamon, and kosher salt and set aside. Toast the bread slices until golden brown. Spread a generous amount of maple butter on each slice and top with a sprinkle each of walnuts, black sesame seeds, cinnamon, and flaky salt. Serve immediately.

MAPLE TOAST

8 tablespoons unsalted butter, at room temperature

2 tablespoons plus 1 teaspoon maple syrup

1/8 teaspoon ground cinnamon, plus more for topping

1/2 teaspoon kosher salt

Fluffy Cornmeal White Bread (page 39), cut into 8 thick slices

Chopped toasted walnuts for topping

Black sesame seeds for topping

Flaky salt for topping

Makes 8 servings

About the Author

Frankie Gaw is a food writer, photographer, and designer. He has worked as a product designer for companies such as Facebook and Airbnb while founding his food blog, *Little Fat Boy*, which was nominated for a Webby and has won Saveur's Blog of the Year award and IACP's Individual Food Blog Award. Raised in Cincinnati, Ohio, he now resides with his partner, Scott, in a quaint home in Seattle, making dumplings and pottery.

Thank Yous

It's the day before my manuscript is due, and this is the last thing I have to write. I can't believe I've made it to the end, to a finished book that only existed in my wildest daydreams between the clicks of a mouse during my nine-to-five job. To type these last words is to close a chapter on a process that has been so fulfilling, one that I don't want to end. The words *thank you* cannot describe the overwhelming gratitude I have for all those who've lifted me up as I've gone along this wild adventure of writing a cookbook.

I'm forever indebted to my two grandmas, my 婆婆, who is still with me today, and my 奶奶, who went to be with my dad while I was writing this book. Thank you, 奶奶, for calling me every week since I was five, and for all those conversations and meals that taught me the love language of food, undoubtedly keeping me connected to my roots even if I wasn't ready yet. Thank you, 婆婆, for the countless FaceTime calls filled with your face too close to the camera. These pages are filled with the countless recipes you taught me, every technique and dish I've learned since I was a kid forming the backbone of this entire book. How lucky I am to have grown up with such tradition, all beginning at the little kitchen island in Ohio when we lived together. I can't help but recognize that the freedoms in my life only exist because of the both of you—your amazing will to survive and make a better life for your family despite the traumas and poverty you've all experienced. For that, I'll be forever grateful.

To my mom: thank you for loving me for who I am and for teaching me to never take life too seriously. I would never have been at a place to pour my heart and soul out for people to read without the unconditional love you've given me. Every photo you post happily posing with a drag queen and dancing at a Pride parade, despite its contradiction to your beliefs, has taught me that God really is just love.

To the rest of my family: thank you for providing an environment filled with laughter amidst adversity. A special thank you to my Aunt Jay, who was so incredibly generous with her time helping me translate my grandma's recipes, providing a breadth of context around family dishes, sending me her entire library of vintage Taiwanese and Chinese cookbooks, and helping me interview my grandma through FaceTime calls. Thank you to my Uncle Jerry for lending his cooking expertise and tips for some of my most nostalgic dishes.

To Sally: I'm so thankful that our paths crossed. This book exists because of you. Your unabashed enthusiasm and mind-blowing expertise have made my dreams a reality while making this entire process the most enjoyable roller-coaster ride that I don't want to get off of. You've been a believer in me since day one, even when I couldn't really see it myself. How did I get so lucky?

To the team at Ten Speed: Thank you, Emma, for being my fairy godmother of cookbooks. You've been a champion of my vision while making the book so much better with your generous input and voice. Lizzie, you captured the vision of this book so beautifully. I nearly passed out when I saw the first designs. The thoughtfulness and creativity you've put into this project from the beginning are a testament to your talent. Thank you for choosing to work with me and lending your creative genius to this book, despite the risks of working with a blabbering former designer with too many opinions. Allison, thank you for your marketing prowess, and most of all for believing in me so early on. To Kim and Carey and Rachel, thank you for helping me get to the finish line, and taking such care and thoughtfulness with these words. Thank you to the entire team at Ten Speed; it's been such a dream to work with each and every one of you.

To 204, my close friends, and my recipe testers: thank you for being my earliest fans and my biggest cheerleaders.

Thank you to my partner, Scott. Where do I even begin? This all started when you had me write out my dreams. It was December 2017, and I scribbled that I wanted to write a cookbook. You had me work backward, visualizing all the things I had to do to get there. It felt like a pipe dream, but five years later it's come true. Thank you for giving me the tools to believe in myself and supporting me during every moment of joy and failure along the way. Your belief in me has literally given me the energy to make it through writing this cookbook. Making me breakfast every day while I was writing this book, despite your early-morning meetings. All those dinners you cooked when I was too exhausted to even touch another saucepan. Every pep talk that gave me the motivation to keep going. I'm so grateful that I get to come home to this life we've built together, a life filled with unconditional love that I never imagined I could find. Thank you for everything.

Lastly, thank you to my dad, my 爸爸. I miss you so much, and I hope I've made you proud.

Index

snapper
Whole Steamed Fish, 178
soups
Creamy Corn Soup, 35
Hangover Chicken and Vegetable Soup, 13
Pork Belly Mushroom Shumai in Corn Soup, 150
Pork Bone Broth with Rice, 111
Taiwanese Beef Noodle Soup, 97
soybeans
Soy Milk, 21
soy sauce, 10
Almond Soy Glaze, 11
Soy and Scallion Sauce, 11
Spicy Soy and Scallion Sauce, 11
Spam
Childhood Fried Rice, 115
spreads, store-bought, 10
squash
Butternut Squash and Pork Guo-Tie, 145
for hot pot, 187
Warm Sweet Potato and Zucchini Shredded Salad, 30
staples, store-bought, 10
stocks
Chicken Stock, 12
for hot pot, 186
Pork Stock, 13
Simple Vegetable Stock, 13
striped sea bass
Whole Steamed Fish, 178
sweet potatoes
for hot pot, 187
Warm Sweet Potato and Zucchini Shredded Salad, 30

T
Taiwanese Beef Noodle Soup, 97
taro, for hot pot, 187
tea
Oolong Milk Tea and Almond Rice Crispy Treats, 200
Soft-Boiled Tea Eggs, 24
tian mian jiang, 10, 95
tilapia
Whole Steamed Fish, 178

tofu
Classic Vegetable Guo-Tie, 141
for hot pot, 187
tomatoes
Cincinnati Chili with Flour Noodles, 101
Fan Tuan with Tomato Egg, 46–48
Mom's Tomato Seafood Stew, 174
Stir-Fried Rice Cake Bolognese, 98
Stir-Fried Tomatoes and Eggs with White Rice, 104
Taiwanese Beef Noodle Soup, 97
turkey
Lau-Kee Congee, 107

V
vegetable oil, 10
vegetables
Classic Vegetable Guo-Tie, 141
Hangover Chicken and Vegetable Soup, 13
Simple Vegetable Stock, 13
See also individual vegetables
Vinaigrette, Balsamic Miso Scallion, 34
vinegars, 10

W
wonton fold, 133

Y
youtiao
Fan Tuan with Tomato Egg, 46–48

Z
Zhá Jiàng Miàn (Hand-Cut Noodles with Minced Pork Sauce), 95
Zucchini Shredded Salad, Warm Sweet Potato and, 30

Typefaces: Grilli Type's GT Alpina and 205TF's Muoto

Library of Congress Cataloging-in-Publication Data
Names: Gaw, Frankie, author.
Title: First generation : recipes from my Taiwanese-American home / Frankie Gaw.
Description: First edition. | California : Ten Speed Press, [2022] | Includes index.
Identifiers: LCCN 2022015031 (print) | LCCN 2022015032 (ebook) |
    ISBN 9781984860767 (hardcover) | ISBN 9781984860774 (ebook)
Subjects: LCSH: Cooking, Chinese—Taiwan style. | Asian American cooking. |
    Taiwanese Americans—Food. | LCGFT: Cookbooks.
Classification: LCC TX724.5.C5 G39 2022 (print) | LCC TX724.5.C5 (ebook) |
    DDC 641.5951—dc23/eng/20220419
LC record available at https://lccn.loc.gov/2022015031
LC ebook record available at https://lccn.loc.gov/2022015032

Hardcover ISBN: 978-1-9848-6076-7
eBook ISBN: 978-1-9848-6077-4

Printed in Italy

All photography and illustrations by Frankie Gaw

Editor: Emma Rudolph | Production editor: Kim Keller
Designer and art director: Lizzie Allen
Production designers: Mari Gill and Mara Gendell
Production manager: Jane Chinn
Prepress color manager: Nick Patton
Copyeditor: Carey Jones | Proofreader: Rachel Markowitz | Indexer: Ken DellaPenta
Publicist: Felix Cruz | Marketer: Monica Stanton

10 9 8 7 6 5 4 3 2 1

First Edition

Featured artists

CHRISTIAN PALINO, *ceramics* • KATIE KRATZER, *textiles* • ERA CERAMICS, *ceramics*
KATIE VON LEHMAN, *ceramics* • THE WAX APPLE, *props* • KESSLYR DEAN, *textiles*